MEGAN'S BOY

AMANDA AUBREY-BURDEN

ISBN:9781723712609
ISBN-13:9781723712609

DEDICATION

I think I was born to box. I've been in the gym since I was 8 years old. My mother Megan had enough of me scrapping in the street and in school and decided to send me to the gym.

I've been involved in Boxing since, and that was 1972. I will always be thankful for her wise decision as I'm sure that Boxing has kept me on the right side of the law, well most of the time anyway.

I spent many years working on the doors in Cardiff, Newport and Chepstow, so inevitably I've had a few fights, in fact I've had a lot of fights - and I like to think I've retired now at age 53 and undefeated on the street.

Boxing is my life, but I'm no statistician or armchair fan. I'm not into facts and figures, I'm into fighting.
Results are important to me and I've had some great ones; Amateur, Welsh, British, Commonwealth, European and Olympic success - along with Professional Welsh, Celtic, British, Commonwealth, European and World Titles.

So many amazing stand-out moments that I wish my mother Megan was around to boast about and boast she would! I'm now a husband, father, grandfather, uncle, brother, and coach - but I'll always be Megan's Boy.

With special thanks to the other Mrs Borg; Emma, my wife, who has been a rock for me at numerous times over the years.
Tony Borg.

.

CONTENTS

ACKNOWLEDGMENTS

Thank you to everyone who has contributed to the writing of this book. The stories, the anecdotes, the memories, precious - one and all, and without which this book would never have been written.

Most heartfelt thanks to **Nikki Brookman**, my literary right-hand – literally! For the countless hours she spent editing and proof-reading my work with attention to detail I could only dream of. Nic is a 'boxing mother', her son Jordi has just embarked on his amateur career and you will often find both at the gym. She is also an academic, and after meeting by chance, a friendship was born which couldn't have happened at a better time and her support has been insurmountable. A friend for life **- Thank you!**

Special thanks to Sharyn Donnachie of *CAPITAL CABS *(Cardiff) and Richie Kane of *FELTFAB *(Newport) for their unstinting and continuous support of St. Joseph's and for sponsoring the launch of this book. Thank you, also, to *FIGHT N FIT *of Bristol for your fab support!

Thanks to WE WILL DO ANY MORTGAGE (Barry) CHAMP BOXING (Torfaen) PENTALK LAB (Newport) CAMELOT FILMS (London)

Thank you also to Dave Harris of **BEBA** British Ex-Boxers Hall of Fame and good luck with your new charity ****RINGSIDE REST & CARE****

*** Last but by no means least, a BIG thank you to Emma Borg! It can't have been easy having another woman delve so deeply into your husband's past, but then she is no ordinary woman. As anticipated, she dealt with it with her usual grace and for that I am most grateful. **Thank you, Emma.**

..

i

ROUND 1 THE EARLY YEARS

When I met Tony Borg in our first year at Willows High it was 1976, little did I know that I would be writing his life-story over forty years later! What makes it more interesting is that we didn't see each other for a very long period of time before social media closed the gap. He came to my first book launch in 2016, and the rest, as they say, is history.
I have to say that he hasn't changed much. The afro may have gone, but the no-nonsense approach to life is still very much there, as is his innate refusal to suffer fools gladly. He was, and will always remain, his own person, and it is that quality that has taken him from sassy schoolboy to successful sportsman – and what a sojourn it's been!

Like Tony, my roots originated in the old Tiger Bay. We both come from an ethnic background and grew up on the same Cardiff streets where children of mixed race were quite rare.
My father, Jackie Chambers, coached for Billy May at the old YMCA, before running Driscoll's Gym above the Royal Oak on Broadway.
He was also best friend and brother-in-law to Joe Erskine, former Heavyweight Champion and one of the many sporting

heroes of Butetown.

Jack worked with Tony briefly when he first turned professional, but prior to that their paths would meet regularly on the amateur circuit and they enjoyed a close bond.

My brother, Rob, who was two years older, also held the title of Welsh Schoolboy Champion around the time Tony had his, so I grew up in a house enthralled to the 'Sport of Gentlemen', where sparring with the gloves – on or off! – was the norm.

As we embarked on this project several things happened, the timing of which couldn't have been better – Tony finally got hitched, and then just days afterwards he received the most amazing accolade.

He's been through the highs and the lows, hit rock bottom and risen again – and again – until we see him as he stands before us now.

An award-winning coach with a stable full of fine boxers whose achievements have made the world sit up and take note of Wales, and what we, as a nation of fighters, have always had to offer.

It has been one hell of a journey for this street-savvy scrapper from Splott, a regular rag to riches saga, but something tells me it isn't over yet.

And so his story begins...

There was no hesitation when Tony was asked what title he wanted for this book. With an impressive career spanning over forty years in the ring, he could've had his pick of a whole array of more grandiose titles. Yet his choice clearly shows that despite all of the plaudits, publicity, and the triumphs, at the heart of it he still is and will always remain – Megan's Boy.

Megan was his mother, an indomitable spirit and the driving force who insisted that Tony don the gloves in a bid to stop him fighting on the streets – often a precursor for many a young boxer and Tony was no exception.

His story begins in 1964 when he was born in St David's Hospital, Cardiff. By the time he'd come along Megan had separated from her husband, a merchant seaman from Malta and was staying with her sister, Menna, in George Street, Butetown. Tony was given the name 'Borg', as were all his siblings, but he never knew his real father, or questioned his paternal side until he was much older when began a growing desire to know the truth.

There was a strong indication that seemed to suggest his father was of Afro-Caribbean extraction and that Tony himself was half-black. Megan, however, would never be drawn and insisted Tony was half-Maltese. Sometimes she would get distressed at his questioning, and not wanting to upset her any more than was necessary, Tony would drop the subject.

Megan, who was to have such an influence on her son, hailed originally from the sea-side town of Pwllheli up in North Wales. She had moved down with her Welsh-speaking parents, Evan Dafydd Evans and Elizabeth, along with her three other sisters when they were very young. As was common at the time, Tony's grandfather had moved south looking for work and soon had the family settled in Cardiff whilst he grafted on the docks.

By the time all four daughters came of age, married and had children of their own, Evan and Elizabeth parted ways.

Evan moved to Portmanmoor Road in Splott, and when Tony was about two years old Megan took a house in nearby Bridgend Street along with his sisters, Jeanette and Lorraine.

 It was here that Tony made his first friend Patrick Evans; both were not much more than four years old at this time and their friendship endures to this day.

Patrick recalls how some of the houses on their street were so old and dilapidated there were still gaslights on the wall and the rich ethnic diversity of its occupants. He also remembers Megan well, and his love for her spaghetti bolognaise. Equally, Tony enjoyed the boiled bacon and spuds that were served up courtesy of Patrick's father, and when both boys weren't in each other's houses you would find them riding the trains down at Splott sidings!

But it wasn't all fun and games and as Tony grew older Evan insisted that he became a regular visitor, so he could gain, as he saw it, some much-needed male influence in his life. This was a mixed bag for Tony. Whilst he enjoyed spending time with his grandfather, the house however, was old and drafty with just one coal fire and no creature comforts. It became a trial of endurance just to go there every weekend, but Evan insisted, and Megan complied. It was one less mouth for her to feed and she recognised the importance of her only son deriving some benefit from the only father-figure in the family.

Jeanette remembers these early days and the hardiness of her grandfather. He was something of a character but did have a soft spot for his black Labrador and Megan's boy, whom he likened to "his eyes".

Evan had little time for the girls, so at weekends when Tony was with his grandfather Jeanette would be sent to stay with their Nan. By this time Elizabeth had thrombosis in her legs and could no longer walk so Jeanette kept her company and has fond memories of a kindly old lady who would occasionally speak in Welsh.

Maria Gooding (*née* Pace), Tony's cousin, also remembers these times and the tough love of Evan. Often when she'd call by Portmanmoor Road she would find Megan's boy toiling away with one chore or another after school. She showed him kindness whenever she could, which has since been returned a thousand-fold by Tony and their special bond endures to this day.

Another relative by marriage at that time, Mary Monaghan, also recalls Tony's early years and speaks of a happy little boy full of mischief. On the odd occasion Mary would babysit the children so Megan could enjoy a rare night out and a game of bingo.

Checking in on Tony one night she was shocked to see tufts of hair scattered all over his pillow. Upon enquiring how this came to be, Tony's explanation, delivered with all the wide-eyed innocence he could muster, was that someone must have cut it as he slept!

He was as endearing as he could be naughty, plainly adored his mother as he was by his sisters, and they were an extremely close-knit family. Money was tight, and life was tough, but everyone pulled together including Megan's siblings, Violet, Mary (Menna) and Gladys.

Christmas's were particularly happy when the four sisters and their children would gather together at the house in George Street. As the adults played cards the older cousins would keep an eye on the younger ones, and the atmosphere was always lively and full of laughter. Megan particularly enjoyed these festive get-togethers – a far cry from her seasonal job of wrapping an endless succession of Christmas trees which would leave her hands green for weeks!

By the time Tony was six or seven years old, it soon became apparent that he had inherited his grandfather's natural feistiness – and Evan was keen to nurture it! But whereas Evan Dafydd had learned to channel his aggression courtesy of the army, Tony, however, had no such discipline and was forever getting into scrapes on the streets. Because he was small, his grandfather, keen to ensure that he could take care of himself often pushed him into confrontations with bigger boys whenever the opportunity presented itself.

This only served to fuel an already fiery nature, so by the time Tony was enrolled in primary school he knew how to use his fists.

This became apparent soon after the family moved from Bridgend Street up to Topaz Street which saw a change in schools. Tony was pulled out of Moorland Road to attend St German's which was much nearer to the new address and there he stayed for two years.

But Tony could no sooner keep out of fights than the sun could remain behind the clouds and Megan knew that something had to be done.

Megan and her best friend, Tessie Sidoryck, arranged for Tessie's son Michael, to take Tony down to Benny Jacob's boxing gym. The plan was that Tony be given a good 'grilling' from resident coach and ex-boxer Phil Edwards. Benny's gym sat at the top of Bute Street and both he and his gym were well known. He was a bookie and ex-fighter, a lively character who had managed the cream of Cardiff champions in their day – a list that included Joe Erskine, Phil Edwards himself, and Lennie 'the Lion' Williams to name but a few.

When Tony first stepped into his gym it was to see Tommy Glencross, British Featherweight Champion at that time, training with all the fervour of a seasoned fighter and from that moment Tony was hooked!

His attention was further cemented by a good talking-to from Phil Edwards who duly fulfilled his word to Megan and took her young brawler to task. In no uncertain terms he berated Tony for street-fighting and suggested he take up the gloves and fight like a 'real man'!

It had been a successful visit and fired up with enthusiasm Tony was keen to go back.

After his second visit, instead of going straight home Tony had been distracted by the delights of the local youth club and had returned home so late Megan put the blocks on.

It was to be a short-lived break, however, when a week later an alternative venue was found that was much nearer to home. One of his neighbours Stephen Huet, Welsh schoolboy champion at that time, suggested Tony try out his gym in Nora Street. And so began his boxing career at Roath Youth ABC and long association with its trainer Gerry Watts that was to last for seventeen years.

Tony recalls his first visit and how he stood out in the street for ages not realising that the garage doors that led to the gym upstairs *was* the only the way in, as he does the smell and the sounds of those working the gloves and how these sensory delights pulled at him deeply and still do to this day. Eventually someone came out who turned out to be Maurice O'Sullivan, ABA Flyweight Champion in that year (1972) who was to reclaim the title two years later; he was also the Olympic Rep. He instructed Tony to go through the dingy garage up the stairs and ask for Gerry.

As Tony stepped into the gym he had his first glimpse of where he was to spend the next few years honing his skills and the sight that met him was a memorable one.

Imagine, if you will, a room, not large but every available

space filled with sweating, sparring, skipping bodies as young boys were put through their paces from the benches to the bag. The ring took up the lion's share of the space, and as Tony sought out and introduced himself to Gerry Watts he was greeted with the words, 'Can you fight?'
'Yes, I can.'

It soon became apparent that Gerry Watts ran a tight ship. He had no time for 'lightweights' or 'slackers'; either you were there to box, or you could find your way out. This level of discipline came as a bit of a shock to Tony, serial street-scrapper with a wild streak, but he immediately felt a connection to Gerry and respect swiftly followed.
He still couldn't help getting into scrapes, however, and retrieving his football one day in the playground Tony was kicked in the face by another pupil. Megan's boy responded in the only way he knew how and there followed a fight whereby Tony got the better of his assailant.
This didn't go down well with the boy in question, who also happened to come from a large family. By the time home-time came around the following day, Megan's boy found a veritable posse waiting for him outside the school gates.
There then followed an exchange between Tony and one of the older brothers who wanted to ascertain exactly what had happened.
Impressed with Tony's stance and obvious fighting abilities, a truce was duly called that in turn saw a sudden influx of would-be boxers flood Roath ABC! It was great for Gerry, who was ever on the look-out for new talent, but the school board at St German's were less than taken, and Tony was promptly expelled.

He returned to Moorland Road and it was here that he made

his first female friend, Donna Goodall, now one of the directors of Cardiff's Motorsearch Magazine. Her lasting memory of Tony is of a small, friendly boy who would chatter on about boxing. She recalls how impressed she had been with his character – and he certainly had plenty of that! But what makes their association particularly poignant is that Donna still had the two boxing badges Tony gave her over forty years ago and recently came to the gym to present them to him.

Back in those days Tony still got into the odd fight, but Megan refused to lose hope and her faith was soon rewarded as Tony began to settle down. Her boy had finally found his niche.
Five nights a week he would pass through the dilapidated garage doors and up the stairs to be put through his paces. It was to be the start of a promising career that would take him beyond the streets of Splott to international arenas, and his training began in earnest.

Here he renewed an acquaintance with Tony Khan, who was two years older than himself. They had met in Splott park briefly a year or so previously, little knowing that they would eventually become friends and regular sparring partners in time. Khan recalls these early days and how well Tony thrived beneath Gerry's stern tutelage.
The two Tony's often sparred together as Megan's boy began to develop his technique. Fleet-footed and strong, he had no qualms getting into the ring with the bigger boys like Darwin Brewster, (nicknamed *Pele*) Steven Huet, Gary Pemberton, Maurice O'Sullivan and Marcel Herbert. Interestingly, and most poignantly perhaps, is that Roath ABC is now run by Tony Khan and Marcel Herbert along with fellow-coach Gary Pemberton as the legacy of its

founder goes on.

But back in the day, Roath ABC had entered into a golden age producing successful amateurs and Welsh Schoolboy Champions. Indeed, the gym was so popular that shower-time would see up to half a dozen bods crammed in under one shower-head, unless *Pele* appeared, whose presence would always ensure a swift exit! The pecking order was strong in those days and Darwin Brewster, as one of the older, bigger boys duly accorded respect so he could shower alone.

Fight-nights were always a cause of great interest and the Roath Labour Club just down the road a particular favourite for local tournaments. In the weeks leading up you would see the young competitors touting their tickets around the streets as the excitement grew.

These events were always well-supported by friends and families, and it wasn't long before Tony was desperate for his debut in the ring. But due to his small stature finding a suitable opponent was proving to be difficult.

He would be taken along to all the tournaments in the hope of finding a suitable opponent, yet when a possible match was found in Newport the doubt was palpable as the boys were put back to back.

Not only was the other boy a lot heavier, he also towered above Tony and Gerry dismissed the idea on the spot. Tony, however, was not fazed by the extra inches or the weight disadvantage and begged and badgered for the chance to prove his mettle.

Gerry finally capitulated, and the match went ahead at 7.30 pm that evening. The year was 1972 and Tony was just eight years old. His challenger was a Newport boy called Godfrey Carneghie, and despite putting up a brave and vigorous fight Tony lost on points.

Tony's first bout in the ring had been an exhilarating experience, yet it had also come as a bit of a shock; it was one thing to spar with bigger boys, quite another when the 'gloves came off' competitively.

But it didn't deter him. If anything, it fired him on, and soon he was boxing his way through a whole medley of tournaments before emerging years later with no less than 105 wins and 10 defeats out of 115 fights. Gerry, however, was of the stalwart opinion that it was actually 107 wins, but it was an impressive record nevertheless!

Megan would attend as many of her boy's tournaments as she could, often with his sisters in tow. Amelia, their first cousin has many fond memories of Megan and her impassioned extortions whenever Tony fought.

With a mixture of threats and the promise of rewards, she would roar like a lioness as Tony, often only hearing his mother's voice amidst the crowd, would duly box to a win. One such instance Amelia recalls is when a bout came up that clashed with a desire to go to Barry Island, the nearest any poor family could get to enjoy the delights of a beach in those days – and Tony had got it into his head he wanted to go.

Megan equally determined that her son would not, dangled the trip like a proverbial carrot, and after getting Tony into the ring, extolled the delights of the seaside until he boxed his way to victory and to Barry Island they did go!

Confrontations continued to happen outside of the gym, however, when Tony moved up to high school. Despite channeling his energies into a more controlled form of combat, trouble still found him and in unexpected ways. He wasn't long into his first year when it came to light that Jeanette was being bullied by a class-mate at school and things had peaked after a verbal attack in the street.

In the spirit reminiscent of her late father, Megan told Tony to deal with it. As the person concerned was two years older and three times the size, naturally there was some reluctance on his part. But Megan was hell-bent and told Tony he was not to come home until the job was done.

The next day after school he sat on the wall outside and waited.

His nemesis soon came along as did Jeanette and there then followed the inevitable shouting match. As things escalated a crowd had gathered and Tony knew he could remain passive no longer.

He left the wall and came forward only to find the hand of his sister's tormentor planted on the top of his head before he was pushed away like some pesky little boy.

It was enough.

Enraged beyond belief Megan's boy launched a volley of shots before the bully knew what was happening and that element of surprise gave him the edge he needed. It also had the desired effect as the bigger boy got the message and Tony could now return home.

Megan's boy had shown his mettle. He was just eleven.

But it didn't end there...

Summoned to the headmaster's office the very next day he found himself being soundly berated. The fact he had been defending his sister and that the boy was much bigger than him was deemed irrelevant, and despite Tony's protests he had his first taste of the cane.

Megan, when she found out, exploded with all the force of Mount Vesuvius! The following morning as we were sat in a classroom that looked out on to the school-yard, we were distracted from our lesson by an extraordinary sight. A woman was striding down the yard with barely-suppressed fury, and as Tony groaned we immediately made the connection and were agog. Megan had arrived, and she was on the warpath!

The whole class began to buzz excitedly as the teacher called for order. A mother had come 'up the school' but not just any mother - this was *Tony's mother!*

Her message, delivered directly to the headmaster, left neither he nor the rest of the teaching staff in any doubt: *Lay a hand on my boy again and there'll be hell to pay!*

Again, it didn't end there.

Some weeks later Tony got into another fracas and once again the headmaster hauled him in for the requisite punishment, despite Megan's warning.

That night as soon as Tony got in from school his mother's first question to him was whether he'd been given the cane. Tony, for fear of what she would do if she knew, said he'd just been given a telling-off, but the truth came out!

Fortuitously for us, our class just happened to be in the same room the next day as a familiar figure suddenly strode into view. As Megan marched down the school yard Tony cringed as inwardly we cheered, because it wasn't everyday you'd see a parent step up to the plate with such vigour! Suffice to say we'd have given our *eyeteeth* to have been a fly in the headmaster's office that day!

The storm finally abated, but controversy was never very far behind Tony, and despite these trials and tribulations school life for him was often fun.

Training for two hours five nights a week, however, was not so enjoyable and he hated it with a passion. Yet his love of the ring was more than a match and he kept the faith taking his cue from one of the most successful boxers of his time, Olympic Champion 'Sugar' Ray Leonard.

Tony himself was a natural fighter and an adept counter puncher, and these two sides came together beautifully as he boxed his way victoriously up to senior level; but it came at a price. Maintaining ideal body weight was a battle in itself and Gerry was often on the case to ensure his young champ didn't go over the required 45 kilograms.

Unlike today, whereby Tony keeps a well-stocked fridge in St Josephs, guidelines back then were so strict that no food or drink was allowed in Roath gym under *any* circumstances!

He recalls one particular incident of abstinence that is as amusing as it is tragic when just days before a fight Gerry pulled out all the stops after Tony weighed in 3lbs over the weight.

Drastic action was called for and Gerry had just the ticket! Just across from the gym was a 'Massage Parlour' and seemingly oblivious to the additional services available therein, Gerry marched Tony across to make use of their sauna. Those spare few pounds were coming off and he didn't care how!

For a young teenage boy to be thrust into such an establishment was toe-curling enough, but as they crossed over the threshold Tony's embarrassment peaked as he recognised the receptionist. It was one of his neighbours and he didn't know where to look!

Inwardly he cringed as Gerry took control and began to negotiate for a session in the steam-room. Despite the fact Megan's boy was not their usual clientele, the receptionist proved to be more than amenable and soon Tony found himself huddled in the sex-associated sweat-box.

Surely it couldn't get any worse, could it?

It did.

Prior to his arrival at the gym, Tony had committed a

cardinal sin as he'd passed the corner shop. The day was warm, and he was thirsty, and although he was aware that he was carrying excess weight, the call of his body would not be denied – he just had to have something! The temptation of the cold drinks fridge was just too strong and before he knew it he had guzzled a can of cola.

Dehydration is a serious issue for anyone, never mind a sportsperson, but for a boxer it is particularly dangerous as it heightens the risk of brain injury. But this was a different era and if you were to make the weight, then not so much as a drop of water was allowed to pass your lips on pain of your trainer's wrath!

Now as he sat and sweltered in his tiny towel Tony soon became aware of two things; Gerry was still in the building – in fact he could see him from the door-window still talking to the receptionist – and the cola he had drank earlier needed to come out. In fact, it was positively insisting on being released in its recycled form as Tony now faced another dilemma; how to appease his bladder which was now on the point of bursting, without arousing Gerry's suspicions!

He stood up, he squirmed, but Gerry showed no signs of leaving, and faced with this terrible dilemma Tony could stand it no more and relieved himself in the water-bucket used for the coals.

He resumed his seat feeling much more comfortable, but this moment of sublime happiness was short-lived as Gerry suddenly appeared at the window with a new instruction.

"The girl says you've got to use the water in the bucket to make more steam!"

Tony stared at him through the glass.

"The water," Gerry gestured impatiently, "*More steam!* Use the ladle that's in the bucket!"

Tony was mortified. No – not *that!* Anything *but that!*

As Gerry waited Megan's boy froze, torn between obedience and outright rebellion. It was bad enough having to starve yourself until you felt dizzy. It was even worse to be so low on moisture in your body that there wasn't enough saliva left to spit, but *this!*

To subject yourself – willingly – to steam clouds of your own piss, pushed beyond boundaries that surely, no man, not even Megan's boy, should have to endure!

The stand-off was short, but far from sweet, however, as Gerry remained eagle-eyed at the door. There was nothing else for it.

As Tony sat miserably in the ensuing sizzle, he had time to reflect deeply on the indignities he suffered in pursuit of his dream, and how, even the mighty could be brought down by a simple can of pop!

It goes without saying he has never forgotten this sauna from hell and remembers well the stench to this day.

ROUND 2 AND THE GLOVES ARE ON!

School at times could be equally challenging but Tony looks back on his these years with great fondness. Naturally sport came high on the list of his favourite subjects, and by the time he hit secondary school he soon found his athletic abilities were in high demand.

Not just content with slugging it out in the ring, it wasn't long before he found himself on the school teams for rugby, football and baseball - the latter being a particular favourite. Besides P.E Tony also wasn't averse to the academic side and recalls English as being his favourite subject. His enjoyment of the language particularly stood him in good stead on the occasions he felt the need to speak out.

He was a popular pupil, always gregarious with a mischievous streak. There was also never a shortage of female admirers enthralled to his charm, but his usual good humour disappeared one day when one of them committed the ultimate *faux pas.*

We were just weeks into our first year and enjoying the usual banter when a classmate compared Megan's boy to the diminutive figure commonly seen on a brand of jam at that time.

To her it was a meaningless remark, an attempt at school-yard wit, but the effect was both startling and immediate as the brow clouded over, the eyes filled with fury, and all laughter fell away as Megan's boy turned into a male version of the Medusa!

We had never seen this side of Tony before and could only watch with a kind of fascinated dread as the perp visibly withered beneath his thunderous regard. The message was loud and clear – make a reference to his size or his colour and you'd soon know about it!

To my knowledge she never opened her mouth in that way again – and neither did anyone else, for that matter. A line had been drawn and a lesson learned - no one messed with the male Medusa!

As a little anecdote to this story, the old adage of adding insult to injury reared its ugly head many years later when this particular pupil and Tony crossed paths at a school reunion. As is usual at these kinds of events, old jealousies are forgiven as are old grudges, so when she confided to Tony that money was a bit short she didn't need to ask twice!

Happy to help an old school friend, he handed over a large sum of money to whispered words of assurance that she would pay him back.

That was several years ago, and Megan's boy remains fifty quid lighter to this day. Fortunately for her he has chosen to see the funny side, but you can rest assured that should their paths cross again there would be less of the silent stare and more of the sharp end of his tongue!

He may have been small, but he was tough, feisty, and took no nonsense, not even from the teachers, and sometimes his propensity to square up got him into trouble. It wasn't long before he struck up a regular relationship with the cane that was to endure for the rest of his school life. But not even 'six of the best' would deter him when his dander was up. Megan continued to visit the headmaster's office, as and when – and not always when the call came to her! As a mother she never failed to fight her children's corner. The fact there was no father at home saw no slacking in this particular aspect of parental duty, and if Megan wasn't available then big sis was happy to oblige.

Jeanette was very much her mother's daughter and not one to be trifled with. As soon as school was out and if Tony wasn't anywhere to be seen, Jeanette would be on the case immediately and with all the tenacity of a New York cop! Once she'd located his whereabouts, off she'd march and into the classroom she'd go before all but physically retrieving him from beneath the teacher's nose.

Faced with this indomitable display of pupil-power the staff member concerned would usually err on the better side of caution and admit defeat. Suffice to say detention was never a problem for Tony when Jeanette was around.

Complaints about Tony's behaviour were usually triggered by confrontations with staff members, some of whom it has to be said, were less than discerning in how they conducted themselves. An example of this was when one made a highly inappropriate remark to a new kid on the block who had recently arrived from Somalia. In no uncertain terms Tony immediately took her to task in front of the whole class. It was a defining moment and quite unprecedented for the fact *a pupil was telling the teacher off!*

We could hardly believe our ears as Megan's boy held forth and to one of the most disliked members of staff in the whole school!

Realising that this particular student wouldn't be appeased by fair means or foul, the teacher then tried to pass her racist jibe off as a joke. No one was laughing however, the teacher

least of all, when Tony, further incensed by this flimsy
excuse referred to her balding head with all the brutality of a
swift uppercut!

In the shocked silence that followed, one thing was clear;
not all of his combative talents were restricted to the ring
and he could deliver a great verbal punch when required! To
say that the teacher was outraged would be an
understatement and she rose up in fury before ordering him
from the room.

The pupil in question and the recipient of Tony's defence
was Ishmael Egal, better known as 'Smiley', and he
remembers well his gratitude at seeing a fellow-pupil half
his size take up the cudgels on his behalf.

It was to be the start of a firm friendship that soon saw
Smiley a frequent visitor to the Borg household where
Megan would insist on feeding him, despite scraping and
saving to feed her own.

But that was typical of Megan. She would give you her last
crust, and in the endless quest to make ends meet, her
cooking abilities were second to none, her curries legendary!
Smiley recalls a very kind lady with a big smile who liked to
keep tabs on her boy as his popularity grew and his social
circle wider.

Another close friend was Martyn Fowler, whose father,
Tommy, had a fruit and veg stall in town. They met in the
first year of high school and became inseparable - joined by
a mutual love of dancing and chasing girls! Youth discos
were all the rage at the time, and the highlight of any school
week was when a local company in Tremorfa would host an
event on the local industrial estate. There you'd find these
two young bucks getting on down in their best bib and
tucker, for if there was anything else Megan's boy loved

more than boxing it was strutting his stuff!

This became a serious business for the disco-duo when 'Saturday Night Fever' hit the cinema's and I think it's fair to say they gave John Travolta a good run for his money! Every weekend they would preen and groom themselves in Tony's bedroom much to the merriment of Megan and Jeanette who would tease them mercilessly. Not that they cared – there was a certain image to perfect and boy, did they have it!

First there was the white shirt and the pristine matching socks. Next up came the black trousers with a chained whistle that peeped 'just-so' from the front pocket, before they moved on to the final touch... a lily-white hanky dangled carefully from one back pocket, their hair combs in the next.

Thus attired, without doubt, they made for a strange-looking and yet striking pair. Tony was small, dark and topped with a magnificent afro, whereas Martyn was tall, fair with natural blonde hair women could only dream of. They were the 'Ebony and Ivory' of Splott and best you didn't forget it! They would hit the town regularly, underage, and hot to trot and all was good until they went up to Birmingham to stay with Tony's family one summer. Hearing of a local disco one night they duly dressed up and made their appearance looking forward to a good time. As soon as they went in it soon became apparent that the gig was more a youth blues than the usual disco, and Ebony and Ivory stuck out like a pair of sore thumbs! The local youth were far from impressed by their presence and the fact Martyn was the only white boy in the house also didn't help. Suffice to say their double-act was far from welcome and they were chased all the way home!

Like a lot of places, Cardiff had all of the territorial

complexities of the Wild West back in the day, and after their brush with Birmingham you'd think they'd have learned their lesson. However, upon hearing of a disco that was going on up in the suburbs, Tony and Martyn decided to pay a visit along with a few friends including Smiley. The area was not known for being particularly friendly to outsiders, but the call of the flashing lights was too strong and so they hopped on a bus and left the safety of Splott.

As the boys hit the dance floor and busted some moves the girls were delighted with this new influx of talent; the local youth however, were not and tensions began to build.

As soon as the disco finished the gloves, as they say, came off as the local boys jumped them outside. Despite the odds against them, the Splott crew fought back valiantly but they were heavily outnumbered, and Martyn ended up in hospital with facial injuries.

Understandably they stuck a bit nearer to home after that, but it wasn't all fun and fistfights as Tony continued to train each night locked in a constant battle with his weight.

The lack of nutrition was torturous in a growing body and although he wasn't particularly food-fixated, Tony recalls surviving on pieces of tangerine and half-cups of water as being particularly harsh.

His constant war with the scales would see him stuff black bags beneath his clothes before pounding the streets until his feet bled.

These desperate measures give some sense of just how committed he was to the fulfillment of his dreams, often to the detriment of his well-being. The endless succession of prelims and tournaments meant energy levels also had to be kept topped up – a veritable challenge within itself akin to a physical Catch 22. But he was as disciplined as he was determined and frequently went hungry in order to retain his fighting weight.

These deprivations and his dislike of training were, for the most part, the only low points of his amateur years.
Although there was one other incident in 1980, when he lost on points in the British Boys Championships to a fine young boxer called John McBride from the famous Repton ABC. In Tony's eyes, to have lost was bad enough, but what made it worse was that his defeat meant he couldn't go on the ten-day trip to New York with the rest of the winning team. It was the kind of lifetime event that didn't happen often, and Tony was incredibly disappointed to have missed out.
He wasn't looking forward to the call home and at first Megan wouldn't believe him and thought he was pulling her leg. No one lauded his achievements more than his mother, and the fact she had already pre-empted the outcome and told all the neighbours he'd won was the typical response of a proud parent and nothing was out of bounds!

To his acute embarrassment Tony often had to endure all manner of people in the neighbourhood knowing the finer details of his boxing career – usually before he did – such was Megan's faith in her son.
His mother was his biggest fan and had been known to kick off on the rare occasion when Tony lost. One such instance happened when the judges ruled against him at a bout in Bryntirion, Bridgend. Patrick Evans, who was present at the time watched in awe as Megan took the officials to task.
It was one thing to deal with an occasional irate father – but they were visibly fazed before the wrath of Megan. Patrick agreed, however, that Tony had been the better boxer, and applauded his mother's refusal to bow down to the decision without a fight
Victory, however, came swiftly on the heels of this defeat

when Tony went on to win the Welsh and the British
Schoolboy Championships as well as the British Boys Club.
An added piquant to these achievements was that a teacher
had mocked him in front of his peers after Tony had
informed him he wouldn't be available for a sporting event.
Apparently not all of the staff were supportive of his
achievements, but a young Mr Borg had the last laugh when
he returned to school on Monday morning with all three
titles under his belt.

Suffice to say the teacher in question had the sense to stay
on the ropes after that!

Despite the volatile relationships he had with many of the
teachers, however, school days for Tony were for the most
part happy, and he even remembers the exact lines he was
given as punishment for repeatedly talking in class.

*The fact I have to write this shows the folly of talking in
class and continuing to do so after being told to keep quiet.*

Perhaps this particular teacher thought that giving Tony
lines in lieu of the cane would go some way in curtailing his
rebellious spirit, but it was often to no avail and his
resistance frequently exasperated school staff who could no
sooner tame a tiger than they could the son of Megan!

By now the Borg clan had been joined by his youngest sister
Suzanne some years before, and the family had moved to
Tremorfa. When Tony wasn't training or competing for the
school he could be found at some disco or sampling the
delights of the Eastmoors Youth Club. And if you didn't find
him there, he'd be hanging out with his bestie from the
Docks, Carl Actie.

It's quite interesting how these two became friends. Like
Tony, Carl had a reputation for being 'tasty', and there were

those who were keen to see them go toe to toe. Indeed, many individuals tried to actively facilitate a fight, yet despite their best efforts all attempts were in vain.

When the two finally got to speak to each other at (surprise, surprise!) a local disco, they actually found that they got on with each other and agreed a fight wasn't necessary – much to the disappointment of the goggling audience! Friendship grew and it wasn't long before Carl joined Tony in the gym and soon showed potential when he won a Welsh title, but was later out-pointed when he went on to fight in the British Championships.

Marcel Herbert was also still on the scene around this time, and was, himself, no mean talent in the ring, both as an amateur and a pro. The trio enjoyed many an adventure together that involved matching wardrobes and an aversion to car-sharing – but that's for another tale!

Tony looks back on these years with a mixture of bemused wonder, and when I asked what was the highlight of his amateur boxing career, he told me this:

"This was the night I won my first British title in the Derby Assembly Rooms, 1980. I beat Michael Clarke from Devon who was a reigning British School's Champion. My mother had travelled up with my sister Lorraine, and earlier in the day I could hear my name being called and recognised my sister's voice. I walked up the tiered seating and met my mother who had planned for a month to be there as a surprise...Probably the best day of my life."

By 1981 Tony had retained all three titles with the added prestige of never having lost a fight for Wales after his initial defeat. Megan attended as many of his tournaments as she could, but as the sole bread-winner she juggled jobs just to keep a roof over their heads. Knowing this, Tony was also driven by the need to take care of his mother for all of the support she had given him.

Martyn Fowler went to nearly all of his fights and lists the most memorable being at Sophia Gardens, Cardiff, when Tony took the Welsh title after beating an opponent twice his size. Indeed, Martyn records that many of Tony's combatants were much bigger than him, yet despite these discrepancies in height – and sometimes in weight - his success was testament to his sheer determination to win. And it hadn't gone unnoticed.

He was approached by programme-makers from HTV who wanted to feature him in a documentary called 'Turning Pro.' By now Tony was competing and winning in the Senior Championships, but with final exams approaching and a glitch in the filming budget, the proposal was put on hold. At just sixteen Tony was riding on the crest of a wave. Surrounded by supportive family members and friends, he rarely encountered prejudice in the boxing world until one fateful day.

The year was 1981, the setting Heathrow Airport, and things were about to kick off in Terminal 2.

The day had started well enough. He was going on a trip to Germany as part of the NABC (National Association of Boys Clubs), and as the only Welshman to have won the British, he had cause, quite rightly, to feel proud.

It also marked his first foray out into the greater world alone.

As Megan waved him off he had in his luggage an envelope she had given him the night before with strict instructions not to open it until he was on the coach.

True to his word, Tony waited until the coach was pulling out of Cardiff Station before opening his mystery gift.

And what a gift it was!

There must have been forty pounds at least in that envelope, a huge amount in those days, especially for a single mother! But Megan, who already worked all hours to make ends meet, had obviously gone the extra mile so determined was she to reward her boy.

Now he knew why she had made him wait, because both of them knew that he would have refused to accept such a generous amount. The gesture was on a par with when she sold two ornaments some years ago so he could go to the circus.

He was deeply touched. No one was more aware than Tony how hard it was just to provide him with kit, and by the time he found his way through Heathrow to the meeting point, it would be fair to say his feelings were running slightly high. He'd just done the journey from Cardiff alone; it was the first time he'd been in an airport, and he was about to board a plane with a load of strangers with what felt like a King's ransom, courtesy of his mother.

As he approached the group gathered on some stairs he recognised a couple of faces from previous tournaments, namely Angelo de Mor. There was quite a crowd of them including various officials, and as one of them began a roll-call Tony missed his name amidst the chatter.

He caught it the second time however, but before he could respond one of the bigger boys called out, 'The nigger up by there.'

Megan's boy couldn't believe his ears, and as you'd expect he responded immediately!

He stood up and a confrontation ensued as he challenged the derogatory remark and the person who had dared voice it. As they argued back and forth the situation became more heated as the officials tried to play it down and restore order.

They entreated Tony to sit back down. He refused. They tried another tack and assured him the matter would be dealt with once they were aboard the plane. But all pleas fell on deaf ears. Still he would not sit down.

The situation had echoes of that day in the classroom when he challenged the 'wit' of a racist remark . Only now he was cast adrift in a sea full of strangers and not one friend amongst them.

And then the unexpected happened.

A young man stood up. He looked at Tony and then to the officials.

"I stand with him."

The speaker was Bobby Frankham, a talented young boxer from a gypsy background. Sadly, his career was to end controversially some years later - but that was in the future - the time was now, and it truly was a magnificent gesture almost reminiscent of a 'Spartacus moment'!

Tony has never forgotten this man or his show of solidarity on that day and their combined stance certainly gave everyone something to think about!

Unfortunately it was not the best start and things weren't about to get any better.

In the months leading up to this trip Tony had been constantly engaged in the usual battle with his weight. Prior to winning his third Welsh title his weight had been 47kg, but he had been told to get it down to 45kg in preparation for the next round of prelims. And so, the cycle of starvation and dehydration began again, because then there were the quarter-finals and the semis; all of these usually taking place within months of each other.

By the time he took the British title he had denied himself a proper diet for months and the process had been nothing less

than gruelling. The trip to Germany was no jolly. The British
Team were there for training camp and Tony had been given
strict instructions not to go over his weight.

When the team flew out he was already feeling the effects of
nutritional deprivation, and a headache came on that was to
plague him for the duration of the trip. Like his peers at that
time, he was unaware of the dangers of dehydration, and in
amateur boxing during this time the need for constant weigh-
ins bordered on the fanatical.

That evening as the team settled down to eat, Tony partook
of a small bowl of soup as everyone around him tucked into
large portions of various dishes. With Gerry's words still
ringing in his ears he could only look on as his stomach
growled and his headache grew steadily worse.

The next day was the requisite boxing exhibition and
Megan's boy now had a fight on two fronts. The headache
showed no signs of abating and because of this he had the
added worry of taking a head-shot.

But the show, as they say, must go on!

He remembers to this day how he jabbed and weaved around
that ring before going back to his room and lying down, his
head raging.

His thoughts turned to his mother and trainer, and how if
either had been there he would have been able to share what
was happening. But they were thousands of miles away, and
after the *fracas* at the airport he didn't feel comfortable
approaching the officials.

It goes without saying that by today's standards he would
have been taken to hospital and checked out immediately.
But this was back in a 'darker age of boxing' when such
medical considerations were simply not known about.

It's frightening to think of what could have happened, and
Tony is of the opinion that he probably sustained some brain
injury as a result of that incidence. **Therefore, he cannot**

stress enough the need to eat sensibly and maintain good hydration. * Please note that this plea goes out to all up and coming amateurs, professionals and their coaches from Megan's boy himself! *****

Summer came and Megan's boy left school with several O levels under his belt his eyes fixed firmly on a career in the ring. Boxing was in his blood and he never felt more alive than when the gloves were on and that bell sounded.

But he was also savvy enough to know that titles didn't put food on the table and he refused to even consider signing on to dole. He wanted to make a proper contribution and take the financial pressure off his mother.

So when just a week or so after finishing school, upon scanning the local paper Tony hit upon a new career that was as unusual, as it was not expected. A hairdressing salon called 'Circles' in Cathays was advertising for a new apprentice. Tony sent off for it along with a few other applications including the RAF St. Athans. The salon owner was the first to respond and invited him for an interview. It went better than anyone could have expected, and soon the gloves were joined by combs and scissors as Megan's boy began a full-time apprenticeship with one-day release to college.

School pal Smiley was one of the first friends to benefit from this new skill-set and particularly recalls holding his peace when Tony trimmed his afro leaving it lop-sided and elongated. Fortunately the friendship survived and no grudges held as the aforementioned hairdressing skills got better!

It was not the career start he wanted and it would be fair to say he hated it, but he was nothing less than determined to pay his way with the thinking something was better than nothing.

He still trained most evenings as he held on to his dream of boxing professionally, and then, of course, there were the nights out...

Along with the usual suspects and a few others from school, the weekends would see Megan's boy hitting the clubs around town. A regular hang-out was 'Sloanes' where the doormen knew them and so entry was never a problem. After a good night on the tiles they would all repair to Lower Cathedral Road where Smiley had lodgings with his father.

The landlady was a God-fearing and extremely kind spinster called Audrey Shepherd whose hospitality knew no bounds. Every Friday and Saturday night her house would accommodate these extra guests and without demur as they squeezed themselves into Smiley's room.

They didn't always sleep, however – at least not immediately without a few fun and games. Their favourite was to stage ghostly phenomenon by way of props, a *Ouija* board and some unsuspecting sap they'd brought back to the house. And if that didn't amuse them enough, there was always the impromptu *Trick or Treat* when passers-by would be scared out their wits by some figure in a white sheet jumping out at them in a mask!

As these high-jinks played out in the front of her house, Miss Shepherd slept peacefully in the back with her cats, blissfully unaware of the horrors being inflicted upon the local populace!

.

ROUND 3 SORROW AND STRUGGLE

Life was good. He had great friends, an apprenticeship and an exciting boxing career that would take him to the top. And of course, he had Megan who forever cheered him on with all the fierceness of a Mother bear.

But she also had a softer side and was thrilled when Jeanette announced the imminent arrival of her first grandchild, purchasing no less than three prams for the occasion! Without delay she revived her knitting skills and would be found, time permitting, sat quietly in a corner with the requisite glass of pop at her side as the pile of baby-clothes became a mountain.

Sadly, Megan only got to enjoy her grandson for a few short months which made the loss of her mother all the more difficult for Jeanette.

Admitted to the Heath Hospital for a routine gall-stone operation, there shouldn't have been anything to worry about - but something went horribly wrong. A bacterial infection had gone into the wound and significantly weakened by this, Megan then contracted TB.

It soon became apparent that she was very ill and would not be coming home.

On 6th July 1982 Megan, the skilled and selfless captain of their ship left on her final journey leaving Tony and his three sisters behind. This remarkable woman, who had single-handedly raised her family at a time when such lone parentage was frowned upon, had done so with unstinting love and pride for all of her children. She was just 47.

Jeanette and her partner Jim were with her at the end. Tony would have been there too, but for a wrong message that saw him go to his aunt's house instead of the hospital. He remembers that day well and his feelings of stunned disbelief.

Megan: His mother, his best friend and mentor, his most stalwart supporter had gone. It just didn't bear thinking about and her passing was devastating for all the family.

Life would never be the same again, but her memory would live on.

And so it does.

People remember Megan as brave, kind, hard-working and fun. Devoted to her family she also left good friends behind like, Kathleen Huq, Peggy Farrugia, Pat Attard, and an Irish woman called Evelyn who would pay the children to brush her hair. These 'Tiger Bay' women were like 'aunties' to her children and the ties of their offspring are still strong today.

Patrick, Tony's oldest friend, has a poignant memory of this time. He'd called by the house just days after, for what he thought was going to be the usual lively visit. He had no idea that Megan has passed away but immediately knew something was wrong as soon as Tony opened the door.

He was quiet and downcast and Patrick's shock on

hearing the terrible news was only surpassed as Tony led him into the front room.

There lay Megan as though she was sleeping. As was customary, the family had brought her home the night before the funeral and placed her in what she used to call her best room.

Patrick remembers this moment as though it was yesterday. How he struggled to identify the still figure with the vibrant woman he had known, whose sense of fair play and fearlessness had made her such a force to be reckoned with.

The air was heavy with sorrow, and desperate to do something for his oldest friend Patrick persuaded him to leave the house and gave him his first driving lesson. As Tony came to grips with the gears it was a brief respite from what lay ahead. He was just seventeen years old and knew that nothing would ever be the same again - he also knew he was about to embark on a whole different fight if he was to keep his family together.

Everything changed with the sudden demise of Megan and the family was left reeling. One of his mother's sisters, Gladys, had flown over from Australia some weeks before with her daughter, Rita. She, along with other family members, including his Auntie Ayesha, provided invaluable support in the following weeks as Tony and his siblings struggled to come to terms with their loss.

It was a huge comfort, but the demands of their lives eventually called them back, and suddenly finding himself the 'man of the house', Tony wasted no time in assuming responsibility. Between him and his older sister, Jeanette, they were managing to maintain a modest income and keep the family afloat, so he was surprised to come home from work one day and find a woman from Social Services in the house.

They were concerned about his youngest sister, Suzanne. Because she was just thirteen years old, they needed to assess the situation and wanted to ask a few questions. They weren't so worried about Lorraine, who was in her final year in school at that time, but they made it clear, nevertheless, that they were not happy with the current set-up.

Equally, Tony made it clear that he was unhappy with what he saw as their interference, and they left, unsatisfied by his insistence that he had everything in hand.

A couple of days later he came home to find another Social Services officer in the house who also happened to be black. This new development wasn't lost on Tony; she had, in his opinion, been corralled into action so that any possible claims of racism he may make against the Service could be safely diluted. He found this implication quite offensive and made no secret of it.

He explained once more, that despite the fact he wasn't yet eighteen, his older sister and himself were more than capable of providing for Suzanne and that it was in the best interests of the family they stay together.

His argument to prevent his youngest sister from being taken into care had the desired effect and they never heard from Social Services again. Without further ado, Tony took up his new role with alacrity, and naturally feeling even more protective of his sisters there were the inevitable clashes as he laid down the law.

Both Lorraine and Suzanne, now firmly established in teenage-mode and still dealing with the loss of their mother, naturally resisted and it was a difficult period of adjustment. Jeanette especially found it difficult to remain in the house. She left shortly afterwards and began a new life with Jim and their baby in West Wales. Tony, seeing no reason to stay in Tremorfa, exchanged the house for a smaller one in Llanrumney taking his youngest sister with him.

Lorraine was old enough to leave home by this time and duly moved out to begin a new life.

Financially it was a struggle, as pay for a hairdressing apprentice was little more than a pittance, and Suzanne recounts how Tony would regularly walk the four miles to work each day so that she had the bus fare for school. Looking back, she wonders that he did it; the responsibility, the sacrifices, working full-time hours and still training in the gym most evenings, and with no help from anyone. By her own admission, Suzanne was not easy to deal with during this difficult period and Tony was nothing less than strict. Life was now a far cry from all she had known when she could hang out with her friends and when her brother would take her 'apple-nobbing'.

Now they found themselves in a different part of the city where they were strangers in the neighbourhood, and for a young girl who had just lost her mother, it was particularly tough.

As Megan's family slowly eased into a new routine without her, it was also at this time that Tony made, what he candidly recalls as being, one of the biggest mistakes in his life. Due to the sudden life-changing circumstances and fuelled perhaps by a need for distraction from his grief, Tony made the decision to turn professional with immediate effect.

Despite a lack of information, financial backing, and his weight being way off-kilter, the misgivings of his trainer fell on deaf ears. Tony was now more determined than ever to pursue his dream, and with the same tenacity that had brought him his first fight; he forged ahead and obtained his license.

Gerry raised his shoulders and arranged for Tony to meet one of Wales's most affluent managers at that time, Billy May.

Billy had a busy set-up at the YMCA building on The Walk, near Cardiff town centre. He also had a gym in Newport.

A few years previously May had taken on one of Tony's old sparring partners, Darwin Brewster, so he was the natural choice. Tony signed a three-year contract with him, but it was soon to prove a turbulent affair as Tony balked at May's style of management and they butted heads on more than one occasion.

Gerry was still on the scene as Tony's trainer, but the dynamics of this new arrangement had introduced a level of tension that had not been there before.

This soon became apparent when the programme makers from HTV re-appeared all set to film their project 'Turning Pro'. At just eighteen years of age, Tony was exceptionally young to be making such a bold transition and the TV crew were keen to document his story.

This was an exciting development for Megan's boy, and it boosted his spirits considerably; things were on the up, and as far as he and the world around him was concerned, boxing was his game and his star was set.

May, however, had other ideas and tried to pull the plug. Tony wasn't willing to miss out on such an exciting opportunity and wasted no time in making his feelings known. May didn't like being challenged and Tony was equally unwilling to be pushed around.

There then ensued a heated debate that nearly came to blows but was averted by May's head coach, Jackie Chambers.

He quickly got in between them and took Tony aside where he dispensed a word of warning; he understood Tony's frustrations, he told him, but if he allowed them to get to the better of him, May had power enough to put the blocks on any future career prospects.

Tony emerged victorious in the end, however, and got his time on air. Filming went ahead but only on the proviso that fellow-boxer, Tony Rahman, who had recently turned pro, was to be included in the project.

Unfortunately the programme makers had missed out on the first part of Tony's journey, but they were in time to chart Rahman's debut in London when he was defeated within the distance.

It was a brutal awakening for Tony's counterpart who was then filmed on the phone afterwards in tears to his girlfriend; notwithstanding it brought home to Tony just how vulnerable you were when at the mercy of cameras and the public eye!

For him, his days of fighting at featherweight division should have been over as he strove to attain lightweight status. But at this point it mattered little; the moment was here, he'd finally turned professional, and hungered for further success.

It wasn't long in coming – the following year he made his debut against Ken Watson at The National Sporting Club, Café Royal in Piccadilly on 21st March 1983. It was an encouraging start and he went on to win his next three fights.

The first of these took place in the same Piccadilly venue

as his debut, on the 28th April against Mick Hoolison.
The second was in Tiffany's Night Club in Newport the
14th June when he defeated Eddie Morgan.

His fourth victory, against Steve James, was in the
newly-built St David's Hall in Cardiff, but the victory
was a bitter-sweet one due to a series of events leading
up to the weigh-in. The boxing presentation at St
David's was a highly-anticipated and prestigious event.
The bill was headed by Kelvin Smart and Canadian
boxer, Ian Clyde for a World Title eliminator, and
accompanying Clyde was none other than Angelo
Dundee, Muhammed Ali's trainer.

Tony had been pulled in to spar with Smart with the
promise of finding him a fight on the night, and in the
couple of weeks leading up to the event, they came
together regularly in the Cardiff gym.

Tony was naturally orthodox but could lead with the right
if required, and during these sparring bouts he was
instructed to box southpaw.

He recalls one particular session when he felt that his
opponent was becoming too lively. Megan's boy wasn't
going to have that and without further ado he switched
stance. This didn't go down well with May, who'd come
by on one of his rare visits to the gym. But it went even
worse with Smart who angrily pulled back.

He demanded to know why Tony had come out of
southpaw when he was being paid to do exactly that!
Tony, bemused by this assertion, replied that he wasn't
being paid *anything* – indeed he had switched to orthodox
because he wasn't willing to get bashed around the ring.
It was obviously the wrong answer as Smart, really
incensed at this point stormed off before disappearing for
two days.

He re-emerged for the weigh-in, however, as did Tony,

but only as a spectator having refused to fight the replacement they'd lined up for him after his original opponent pulled out.

The replacement was Steve James who was known as 'a big puncher' and Tony, who'd been sparring southpaw with Smart in the weeks leading up, felt the switch back to orthodox would put him at a disadvantage.

After having made his concerns more than clear and his wishes seemingly accepted, Tony had agreed to go along with May and watch the weigh-in.

The date was 29th November and as proceedings got underway, the first sign something wasn't right was when Tony heard his name being called to the scales.

He looked at his manager and May looked away. The officials called out his name again and feeling perplexed, Tony stepped up and explained that he was merely there as a spectator and that he would not be fighting.

The officials took no notice and insisted he step onto the scales but Tony refused.

Because it was a fight for a World title, a TV news crew were filming that evening and seeing some kind of an exchange unfolding, the camera crew moved in for a closer look.

By this time things were getting a little agitated and eventually Tony stepped on to the scales feeling increasingly bewildered. He was one and a half pounds over his 9st 2lbs which in turn caused a stir and Tony went back to his seat, his anger rising.

The officials called him back with one of them making the remark that if Tony didn't comply and get back on the scales he would be pulled up in front of the board and stripped of his license.

It was an unpleasant moment as much as it was a defining

one, and as the camera's rolled, Tony's response became
more heated and he was warned to watch his tongue.
Feeling completely powerless by this turn of events, and
with no one to fight his corner, he knew when he was
beaten and with fury in his heart stepped back on to the
scales; but he didn't do so quietly.

This was an unprecedented moment and the TV crew
asked Tony what was going on. Forthright as ever, his
response was as damning as it was disturbing; he said he
was being forced to fight and that he was angry at his
treatment. He said he felt 'used and abused' and what
was worse was that no one was willing to listen to him.
One of the coaches in attendance, Marlow Offside
intervened and tried to play things down saying Tony was
merely upset because of a headache and hand injury.
Tony was swift to refute it, but the officials eventually
got their way and he felt he had no other choice than to
get into that ring and box.
Megan must have been watching over her boy that night
because he emerged from the ring victorious much to
May's delight. Yet despite this and the flurry of plaudits
from the very officials who had held him to the fight,
Tony continued to be outraged at their tactics and still
hasn't forgiven them to this day.
*Since beginning this project Tony has been able to obtain
a copy of this footage and the contents therein wholly
support his version of events.*

.

ROUND 4 CHALLENGING TIMES

There were already changes happening in other areas of his life during this time. In 1981/82 he had entered into a relationship with a girl from Newport and his first child was on the way. Determined not to emulate the behavior of his elusive 'father', Tony wanted to be a proper part of his new family so he moved to Newport at the end of 1983 taking Suzanne with him.

He still travelled to Cardiff every day and continued with his apprenticeship, but he also started to skip the odd training session as life became ever busier when he welcomed his first child into the world on New Year's Day.

His next fight was just a few weeks later in the most prestigious venue he'd ever fought in, the Lyceum Ballroom on The Strand. This was also to be where he tasted his first defeat at the gloves of Charlie Coke on 26th January 1984.

But it wasn't enough to put our young champ off his game, and during his next fight on the 16th April he caused no small controversy when he knocked Alex Cairney out in the second. The venue was St Andrew's Club in Glasgow, and Tony had seemingly broken one of Boxing's unspoken golden rules when you fight from the away corner.

May had explained to him that traditionally, the understanding was that you were there to box, but not to win. Tony's inarguable success caused something of an uproar on the night, and hearing his manager apologising in the changing room afterwards only further fuelled Tony's refusal to 'play the game'.

His submergence into the professional world of boxing was proving to be an eye-opener, and with no fan-base, parents, or any real support behind him, his mindset was simply to go into that ring and win regardless.

Around this time he had also been put forward as 'Prospect of the Year' but had lost out to Frank Bruno and could only wonder how things might've turned out differently had he received the benefit of the right backing.

His next bout on 13th June against Steve James in Port Talbot saw another defeat, and for any sportsperson who is accustomed to winning, there was more than the sound of the round bell ringing. But Tony pushed on regardless, and on 20th September he'd picked up the pace and defeated Les Walsh in The Wythenshawe Forum up in Manchester.

Just a month later when it seemed Tony might be getting back on top of his game he suffered defeat at the hands of Dave Kenny on 11th October at the Civic Hall in Barnsley. Then on 16th January 1985, he fought and lost to Gary Nickels at the Britannia Leisure Centre. It was a bad start to the year and perhaps a sign of things to come...

The Nickels fight had been somewhat unconventional when Tony kept slipping on the advertising strip that ran across the ring floor. Frustrated beyond belief, there was only one thing for it and he stripped of his boots and socks and fought barefoot for the last 4 rounds.

Despite his best efforts, however, he lost on points, but it was a memorable display that showed dogged determination.

He was soon back on form, however, when he defeated Michael Marsden later that year on the 9th November at the Newport Centre.

The year was drawing to a close and it marked a turbulent period of wins and defeats since his decision to turn professional back in 1982. He looks back on this period of his life with all the sagacity that comes with a wiser head. How he'd jumped straight in. How he'd ignored the inconsistency of his performances. But he doesn't dwell on it unnecessarily. Megan's boy has ever been one who looks to the future.

Life outside of the ring had been ticking by over the preceding years, but 1985 marked several changes in his personal life and early that summer also saw the arrival of his second child.

Just a couple of months later he finally completed his hairdressing apprenticeship and with a distinction, no less! His sense of liberation was immense.

It had been a tough few years keeping his hand in a career that didn't hold his heart - even harder trying to survive on a pittance. But he'd stuck it out, supplementing his income by working the doors around Cardiff which meant long days and even longer nights. Yet somehow, despite all the challenges, he'd done it.

Meanwhile, an offer came in to manage a barber's shop on Tudor Road in Cardiff, and although Tony was reluctant to go back to the scissors, the job paid well, and he had a growing family to support. Living in Newport meant the continued commute to Cardiff each day with training in the evenings.

After six months running the barbers he'd had enough and took a job at Handiland. It had been an eventful year, and despite enjoying support from family and friends, it was not the life that he'd envisaged. Megan's boy was often a restless soul and by the end of the year relations with his partner and mother of his children were no longer harmonious and home-life had become difficult.

As 1986 dawned, little did he know that this next fight was going to be a major turning point - not just for his boxing career, but for the next phase of his life when he stepped into the ring with former undefeated British Champion Steve 'Sammy' Sims.

The date was 23rd May, the venue, Risca Leisure Centre, and all of Tony's work colleagues from Handiland had turned out to watch him box. He was contending to take from Sims the title of BBBofC Welsh Area Super Featherweight, and with his previous win firmly in mind he was feeling fairly confident. Steve and Tony were known to each other and had sparred on numerous occasions at Roath Youth ABC.

Even though Sims was some years older and possessed more experience professionally, he acknowledges that Tony was, at that time, a worthy opponent. He recalls how he would feel an almost comedic sense of dread when he'd hear his step on the stairs, little knowing that Tony entertained exactly the same sentiment as he entered the gym with the thought, *Oh no, not him again!*

At that time Sims was being coached by Roger Williams around the gyms of Newport, and Roger, who had heard about Megan's boy finally got to meet him at the weigh-in. He recalls his first impression and subsequent surprise at his small stature with the words, "He looked like a little boy" little knowing that this 'little boy' would go on to become a close friend and fellow-coach!

Tony fought Sammy over the full ten rounds that night but he lost on points. His ability, however, didn't go unnoticed -

and by his very opponent himself! There was a rapport between them that was to evolve into a new working relationship soon after.

It couldn't have come at a better time. Daily life had become a punishing schedule as Tony juggled travel, work and training. He'd also recently purchased his first house, yet felt he'd reached something of an *impasse* as his personal life became more turbulent. He also continued to struggle with his weight.

Something had to give, and the next bout was the decider. He went up against Mark Pearce in The Star Centre, Splott on the 24th November and it marked another defeat. This was to be Tony's last fight in Super Featherweight division and also his last one under Gerry.

After seventeen years it was time to say goodbye. It was an awkward and poignant farewell - theirs had been a long and successful association, but the world was changing, and Megan's boy was ready to move on.

He made a fresh start under the tutelage of Sammy Sims, who, by his own admission, pushed Tony hard. But there were no complaints. Megan's Boy absorbed the extra training, running up to ten miles a day and Sammy had no doubts he had a champ on his hands.

They began training at Billy May's gym in Newport that was based in the old Father Hill Secondary School, and the future looked bright. They were on their way!

Tony had his next fight on 3rd March 1987 as a Lightweight, but it was marked by his third defeat as he lost to Andrew Furlong in the Porchester Hall, Queensferry.

Just over a month later a fight came up at short notice over in Belfast against Eamonn McAuley in the King's Hall. The match was set for the 25th April, and battling as usual to maintain his weight, Tony had made the trip with no sustenance of any kind.

By the time he made the weigh-in he was, to put it in his own words, "absolutely starving" but he was bang on weight, felt fit, and more than ready to give it his best shot. Tony was ahead on points when he walked on to a heavy right hand and went down in the fourth round. The ref stopped the fight; it was his fourth defeat in a row and a serious wake-up call.

Tony was still determined to make his mark professionally, but he realised he had to 'up his game' by cutting his weight sooner and really knuckling down. His training regime had been erratic for some time; it was now time to *really* 'go to work'!

After training hard all summer, his next fight was set for 15th September against Mickey Crawford whose corner man was Frank Maloney at that time. The venue was the Royal Gardens Hotel in Kensington, and Tony came back with a vengeance.

Crawford took a lashing and the fight was stopped after he took a cut, and this set the pace for the next three bouts that saw Tony back at the top of his game. A month later on 19th October he defeated Ray Newby up in Nottingham at The Albany Hotel.

The next fight was at The Town Hall in Hove the following year on the 26th April and brought another win, this time against Mike Russell. On this occasion Tony shared the dressing room with none other than Chris Eubank, and he still recalls his bemusement at Eubank's unique style of preparation in front of the mirror.

So it was with a certain sense of disbelief that Tony beheld Eubank's rise to fame as his skill and flamboyance took him to the very top as World Champion and with it, the old adage, you should never judge a book (or a boxer) by its cover!

A few weeks later he was back in the ring against Brian Nickels, but not before a rather amusing incident that took place prior to the weigh-in. The event was taking place in The Cafe Royal, Piccadilly, and Tony was in the queue waiting to see the doctor when Sims went off for a walk. He was soon back and told Tony that he'd just had an encounter with Nickels who'd given him 'a look' that resulted in a stare-down.

Greatly amused Tony informed him that it couldn't have been Nickels as his opponent was standing just across the way! It soon became apparent that Sims had been eye-balling a complete stranger, and this case of mistaken identity caused much hilarity and still does to this day. In spite of losing to Megan's boy that night, however, Nickels bears no grudge and he and Tony remain on friendly terms. Indeed, Brian is now a successful stunt-man and fight-arranger in the TV/Film industry.

Next up was Ian Honeywood who was managed by Frank Maloney. The date was 30th August and the venue, the Royal Lancaster Hotel in Bayswater. As the final bell went at the end of the eighth round Tony, confident that he had won, could hardly believe his eyes as Honeywood's arm was raised into the air and he wasted no time in challenging the decision.

He took his complaint directly to Frank Maloney himself who tried to appease him but to no avail. Tony knew his protests were in vain, but he needed to vent his frustration with the assertion that he was *not* 'a Journey-man'.

Winning meant more to him than the money, and it still does over thirty years later.

He came away from that fight furious with the belief that once again any chance of him winning fair and square was being thwarted by what he saw as the old 'home-school-rule.'

On 28th September Tony was back in the ring that saw a feisty performance on both parts when he fought B.F (Robert) Williams at Picketts Lock Stadium, in Edmonton. Williams had several inches on Tony and this showed in the first round when Megan's boy was caught with a left uppercut that took him down. When he returned to the corner, he was unaware that he was bleeding, and thought he'd merely slipped. By the third, Williams showed he meant business and followed through with a blow which resulted in a cut to Tony's eye.

With several rounds to go, at this point things were starting to look a bit worrying and Megan's boy knew he'd have to raise the bar.

This he duly did in the seventh with a barrage of shots that put Williams down with a right and cuts to both eyes.

It was a dramatic and satisfying end to what had been a challenging year, but little did Tony know as he stepped out from the ring that night, he was about to be hit by a series of life-changing events and he wouldn't don the gloves again for four long years.

As a little footnote to this, Williams went on to great success and is now a top Referee and MC.

ROUND 5 DARK DAYS

Life outside the ring could be equally combative as Megan's boy continued to work the doors around Cardiff. Old pal Smiley recalls these days and his debut night under the tutelage of Tony Borg.

It was the end of the night and security were doing the usual sweep. Smiley had asked a patron to finish up his pint only to find himself being given the verbal run-around. As Megan's boy came around on the third check the guy was still nursing his pint as Smiley hovered uncertainly.

Without further ado the fists came out and the man went down.

"Just drag him out," said Tony, "and remember - the next time someone takes the piss, first you ask nicely, the second time more firmly, and if they're still there by the third time you come round just do what you have to do especially if they're giving you lip."

Suffice to say the man he'd knocked clean out had given him 'lip'!

Smiley has since moved on from those days and now enjoys a successful career in the motor industry, but he's never forgotten the no-nonsense brutality of that night.

Unlike the stringent standards of security today, dropping an unruly customer was pretty much standard back then.

Working the doors was often a volatile and risky business but one night the 'norm' got out of hand as Tony and his usual crew took up their positions. A call came in from a neighbouring club – a large Stag party was doing the rounds and their rowdy behaviour was causing some concern. It was the usual heads-up when potential trouble was on its way, and by the time the groom-to-be and his friends turned up, Tony, as supervisor, had already decided the group were not coming in.

The party took umbrage at this decision, but the doors remained firmly shut. Tempers flared, words were exchanged, and as the situation escalated the fists began to fly.

It was to prove a defining moment; a ripple-effect of life-changing events that would make their mark felt for years to come.

In the ensuing melee, Tony's altercation with one of the stag-party ended when he broke his jaw and repercussions followed swiftly on.

Arrested and charged with Grievous Bodily Harm, it wasn't long before Megan's boy found himself up before the Judge at Cardiff Crown Court.

The date was 20th October 1988 and there was a strong possibility he would be sent down.

The Judge, however, took into account Tony's job position as an Assistant manager and the fact that he had a growing family to support and let him off with a heavy fine.

Thankful to have escaped a prison sentence, Tony left the court that day with a huge feeling of relief and hurried home to Newport thinking to go for a run and take stock of all that had happened.

His old opponent and now good friend and trainer, Sims was waiting for him and together they set off on their usual route around Duffryn on the outskirts of Newport. Tony recalls his mood as happy because in spite of the rain, he was out on the street and not behind bars, and as they literally turned for the home-run a car suddenly came out of nowhere and tragedy struck.

Sammy saw the vehicle in the nick of time and managed to get out of the way. Tony, however, was not so lucky. Hindered by the hood on his head he saw and heard nothing but the sound of the rain and his own breathing.

As the car hit him he was catapulted off the windscreen and on to the boot before being thrown across the road.

Unlike some people who have no recollection of a major trauma, Tony recalls everything; the moment of impact, his shock and the absolute agony as he lay helplessly in the road.

Despite ensuing speculation that the incident was in some way a revenge attack related to the court case, the incident was simply pure coincidence. The driver, who was on his way home from work, was practically hysterical and Megan's boy holds no ill-feeling towards this individual - not even to this day.

As soon as the ambulance got Tony to the Royal Gwent Hospital it soon became apparent that in addition to the broken tibia and fibula in his left leg, his lower back had been damaged, as had his right shoulder. He had also sustained a head injury and was slightly concussed.

The hospital kept him in for one week before he was discharged, his entire leg pinned and in plaster. Unaccustomed to such limited mobility, Tony was keen to get back to some semblance of his old life and within days he was hobbling down into town for a night out.

With a friend in tow, he made his way to a nightclub where he was on friendly terms with the manager. The evening passed by pleasantly enough and he was invited to stay on afterwards for a drink. At closing time, one of the doormen, unaware of this prior arrangement became belligerent upon seeing Tony and his friend still sat in the club and demanded they leave. This simple misunderstanding could have easily been cleared up but for the next words out of the doorman's mouth when he made the fatal mistake of using the 'N' word at Tony.

There is one thing that Megan's boy won't tolerate and that is being called *nigger* – and the fact that he was newly-released from hospital full of pins, pain and pent-up passion meant there was only one way this was going to unfold and having just one good leg wasn't going to stop him!

To quote the friend who was with him at the time, "Then Tony stood up like a Japanese swordsman and I thought, *Oh my God...*"

There then ensued a most bizarre exchange as Tony lashed out and delivered a bone-cracking whack before wielding his crutches like well-honed weapons as the remainder of the doormen came at him only to be similarly dispatched. What he couldn't do with his fists he did with his sticks, and as his assailants backed off he hobbled outside with his dignity intact.

The Police, who had turned up by this time, took him to one side and questioned him briefly. He denied all knowledge of the incident, and seeing only a man on crutches, they believed him and let him go, because no one on sticks would have been capable of that, surely...*would they?*

The situation with his leg was to prove troubling and became his *Achilles heel* when it snapped ten days later. Tony was re-admitted to the Gwent for more surgery, and although friends and family rallied round offering support, depression was already setting in at the prospect of months on crutches and what this would mean for his career.

For the first time in his life, Tony felt betrayed by his body as he became dependent on others, unable to work or do the things he loved. It gave him an insight into the difficulties faced by less able-bodied people who dealt with this daily, but he struggled nevertheless and abhorred the fact, that for the first time in his life, he had to rely on state benefits.

It was a crushing blow to someone as independent as he was, so when he got the call to attend a meeting with the British Boxing Board of Control in Cardiff shortly afterwards, he was in no doubt that some kind of reprimand would be forthcoming. There wasn't much you could keep from the boxing world but then the headlines of the local rag, 'Boxer breaks jaw of Stag night reveller' had made sure of that.

As a result of his injuries and ensuing low mood he had already decided to throw in the towel. He just couldn't see a future back in the ring and had lost all interest. So, when he came before the panel in a Cardiff hotel he was already prepared for what they might throw at him.

It was not a welcoming committee by any means. The (BBBofC) British Board of Boxing Control took a dim view of fighting outside the ring and were also operating under the impression that Tony's accident with the car had in some way been a 'revenge attack' because Tony had escaped prison.

He had brought the name of the sport into disrepute, they told him, and a decision had to be made about what they were going to do about it. As the accusations and misinformation kept coming, Tony tried to explain that he'd already decided to resign, hence making their decision invalid; he also didn't care for the way they were speaking to him but his protests fell on deaf ears and soon he could feel his anger rising.

The rigidity of their approach, coupled with the fact he was still on crutches faced with an unknown future, served only to fuel his frustration and matters soon escalated as the board refused to let him speak.

They needed to confer in private, they told him and asked him to leave the room. Tony refused. Eventually he was ushered out as they made their decision before summoning him back with the announcement that he would be banned for 18 months.

He knew it was coming, of course, but the anger that had been steadily building finally erupted and getting up from his chair, Tony hobbled across to the long table behind which the dozen or so officials were sitting and let rip!

Slamming a crutch down on the table in front of them, he launched into a furious tirade of pent-up frustration and insisted they hear him out. His rage was such that even to this day, he freely admits that he 'lost it'.

Their continued refusal to let him speak only served to escalate the situation and security was called in the form of two fellow-boxers, Andy Gerrard and Dai Gardiner.

Both individuals are of particular note. Dai is now a renowned manager and coach who has taken care of Johnny Owen, Robbie Reagan and Steve Robinson to name but a few. Gerrard, a tough Welsh Heavyweight from Risca, near Newport, has come up against some of the world's top heavyweights in his time, but this was probably the most unusual pre-fight stance either of them had ever encountered as Tony dared them to touch him, as outnumbered and as incapacitated as he was.

They both took in the situation with dismay. They knew Tony, of course, and there followed a tense few minutes as they tried to talk him down, but the months of frustration coupled with the Board's dismissive manner had turned into a stand-off.

There was only one thing for it.

Before he knew what was happening Gerrard had sprung into action and came at Tony from behind. Wrapping his arms around him, he lifted him up crutches and all, and removed him from the room!

It was an unprecedented moment, but it had the desired effect as Tony had no choice other than to calm down and compose himself. He then left the building and with a soured relationship with the BBBofC that would endure for the next few years.

Life had changed dramatically, and not for the better. Never a regular drinker, Megan's boy now embarked upon an ill-fated liaison with the dubious delights of 'snakebite'. This infamous mix was well known for exacerbating certain behaviours, and Tony, beset with anger issues was no exception. Unable to train, and live his life as he had always done, his pursuit of a career in the boxing ring was seemingly out for the count and within weeks he was back in court for a fracas in the street.

This time the presiding judge was less lenient.

On 18th January 1989, Tony began the New Year with a three-month sentence as a guest at Her Majesty's pleasure. The shock of finding himself inside the confines of Cardiff 'Nick' was an experience he wasn't to forget in a hurry! The fact he was also still on crutches at this time added no small surrealism to the situation, but it was also a period to reflect and take on board how far he'd fallen from the path his mother had set.

It was a rude awakening as much as it was an enlightening

one and being cooped up with strangers in a ground-floor cell was particularly testing.

He began to keep a diary, and it became his outlet from the daily grind of prison life.

It was the first time he had ever been separated from his children, and he missed both of them dreadfully.

The loss of freedom, being unable to partake in everyday normal life and the complete removal of control all had a sobering effect, and he reflected on his actions with the vow *never again!* But he had learnt much.

Whilst he was there he heard a knock at the door one day and looked up to see one of the Cardiff Five who'd been wrongly arrested for the terrible murder of a young woman called Lynette White.

The case was, and still continues to be, a sensational subject to this day. Not least because all five had been victims of a terrible miscarriage of justice – the details of which didn't fully emerge until many years later when the actual killer was found.

Tony recalls their conversation and the complete bewilderment of the accused. How they sat in his cell and he listened to a man tear his soul apart for something he hadn't done. The anger, the disbelief, the protestations of innocence because by his own admission he knew he'd been no angel, but he wasn't capable of *that!* And what's more he hadn't! He was *not* guilty!

Megan's boy had no doubts of that. Whilst the trial had been going on, Tony had taken time off from his job at Handiland so he could attend every day, little knowing he'd end up sharing jail-time with one of the accused!

But as mentioned previously, the 'Tiger Bay' ties are strong and Tony has never forgotten those dark moments of a man's despair and the sense of vindication when the truth came out when the Cardiff Five were exonerated forever.

Release, when it came, saw him emerge back into the world with less of a chip on his shoulder and a determination to make a new path for himself. His first port of call was home before visiting the hospital and getting his leg-cast removed. Physically he knew he was in a bad place, and mentally he knew he wasn't much better. Depression was a constant companion and a reminder of what he had lost. Dreams of reaching the top of his game were now dust, and so he turned his attention to coaching instead.

The local boxing world was thrilled to have him back but the BBBOFC seemingly less so, and when Tony applied for a Trainer's License they wouldn't even see him and turned him down. Subsequent applications over the next three years were also refused as the spectre of Megan's Boy in all his fury still appeared to resonate strongly with them.

It was a challenging time but not everyone during this time was as unfriendly, and upon bumping into his old boss from Handiland one day the upshot was being offered the manager's position at the store in Newport.

Here he renewed his friendship with Andrew Leighton, a co-worker from his previous position at the firm. Ironically, at this juncture, Tony was now his superior but they simply picked up from where they'd left off as Tony returned to his old tricks.

This would take the form of raiding Andrew's lunchbox and pulling out half of his sandwiches. He would then cough all over them, hence ensuring a free lunch every day as his benefactor would look on with bemused resignation.

Such was life when you worked with Megan's boy...

The steadiness of this position, coupled with regular coaching sessions ensured a slow but steady ascendance back into some kind of normal life, although there remained a nagging distraction that wouldn't go away.

It was during this time he had a taste of what could be achieved, however, when he hooked up with Marcel Herbert. Both of them have a long association and remain good friends from their days at Roath Youth ABC, and despite the BBBOFC still refusing to give Tony his license, he and Marcel went to work regardless.

Marcel had been dipping in and out of the boxing scene for some years and now had Tony acting as his unofficial coach. So, when the call came in for Marcel to fight Steve Robinson, there was no way Megan's boy was going to *not* work the corner!

The date was the 19th August 1989 the venue Splott Market, Cardiff, and Herbert made a memorable debut when he beat fellow Cardiffian Robinson on points.

Marcel was showing himself to be quite tasty and despite a couple of losses, soon found himself in France about to have the most memorable fight of his life!

The date was 12th December 1990, his opponent Super Lightweight, Jean Pierre Scigliano who had won twelve of his thirteen bouts.

As the bell ended the first round, Marcel was never more pleased to see the corner. He'd taken a complete pasting and as Tony mopped his brow Marcel made no bones about the fact he believed the Frenchman was too strong. Suffice to say he wasn't looking forward to the next seven rounds.

But he reckoned without Megan's boy and his infallible faith in all who fight from under his wing. "Go in close to him," he said, "go to him." Marcel did, and by the fourth he'd rallied and was proving to be a worthy opponent.

At the end, much to his amazement he found his arm being raised to the announcement that he was the winner!

Both he and Tony were cock-a-hoop. What a comeback!

What a result! They were made-up, and all fine and dandy until they tried to leave the ring.

The Gallic audience were less than thrilled with the result and had surged forward blocking the way. They began disputing the decision in their usual impassioned way and the situation became heated.

At the risk of being mauled by the mob, Tony and Marcel had been ushered to the centre of the ring as officials battled to restore order.

This was finally achieved with the elimination of the first announcement due to a mistake in the judging. Marcel was no longer the winner. The officials now decreed that the bout had been a draw and that did the trick!

This time as Megan's boy stepped carefully from the ring with his two-minute champion close behind him, the crowd duly parted and let them through.

It was a surreal moment and Tony still marvels to this day that this was allowed to happen, but more tellingly perhaps, is the fact that only he can go to France and nearly start another Revolution..!

Despite the dramas overseas however, Tony was delighted with his coaching role. Here, at last, was a sign that perhaps he had what it took to get the best out of raw talent, and having tasted such success during his amateur years, the hunger was still there for championship status.

As was the taste for action - and if he couldn't attain it through his boxers, then he would have to go back out there and do it himself!

Sammy Sims was delighted at the prospect of his former opponent and one-time *protégée* returning to the ring, and together they devised a training programme that would build Tony back up to fighting fitness.

For the first time in years Megan's Boy felt a new lease of life and despite the fragility of his leg and almost constant pain in his lower back, he persevered and after a particularly good sparring session he knew he was ready.

By now he and Sims had moved premises and were working out of an attic space they'd converted at a car auction site called The Maltings. Their time there was particularly memorable for the occasion when Sims unwittingly bid for two cars whilst trying to get the manager's attention! But it was to be St Joe's that would be the last gym Tony would come out of as a professional boxer.

After four years of turbulence and extremely tough times, he strived still for the dream and worked through the pain of his old injuries, determined to give it his best shot. It was a brave and valiant effort, but little did he know that his comeback would comprise of just three more fights before he hung up the gloves forever. A bout was set for Grosvenor Square, Mayfair, on 16th September 1991 against Peter Bradley who was no mean opponent having recently challenged for the Commonwealth title. Tony and Sammy knew this would be a real test in more ways than one.

It was a close fight and Tony remembers well the great timing and position of Bradley, but he couldn't get near him and lost by a point. He knew he had given a good account of himself, however, when the *Boxing News* came out with the headlines, *Bradley, shaken not stirred* and he looked forward to the next bout.

Next up was Felix Kelly, just two months later on the 20th November at the Star Leisure Centre in Cardiff. This time Tony was determined to win and it was an exhilarating display as both opponents gave it all they had going 'toe to toe' as reported by Colin Jones of HTV.

Emerging from the ring victorious with all aches and pain forgotten, Tony dared to hope that this could be a sign of things to come and when he went back to The Star the following year it was to be his last and final fight.

The date was the 22nd January 1992 and fate once again played a hand when the original opponent pulled out. Tony had been struggling with his weight, and despite embarking on the usual 'fast' he just couldn't shift the extra 2lb he was carrying.

When Sammy put forward Ross Hale as a replacement, the fact that Hale was undefeated didn't faze him, but the aftermath did when he lost on points. Along with this defeat came the realisation that he was never going to fulfil his dream.

He stepped down from the ring that night and knew that this particular part of his journey was over. His back was in agony, once again he'd struggled to make the weight, and besides, one win out of three simply wasn't good enough. As the laces were untied for the final time, he made the decision there and then that his time in the ring was over, and he moved forward setting his sights on a whole new horizon.

ROUND 6 PHOENIX RISING

All his life the gym had shaped him and now it saved him.
The relief of no longer having to starve himself due to the
constant battle with his weight meant that Tony could now
focus his energies on a coaching career. Roger Williams,
who was by this time head coach at St Joe's, asked Tony to
come onboard full-time with the view of offering private
sessions. Sammy Sims was delighted and with their
combined experience their intention was to put St Joe's well
and truly on the map.

Whilst still training Marcel Herbert, another boxer came to
Tony's attention by the name of Alan Ley, one of St Joe's
regulars who was on the cusp of turning professional. By
this time, Tony had finally been awarded his trainer's
license, and under Tony's tutelage Ley had a promising start
with four wins under his belt.

A rude awakening came, however, when Ley was put up
against 'Prince' Naseem Hamed in the Grand Hall at
Wembley 1993.

The latter was a formidable opponent and despite Tony's
warning he would be too strong, Ley insisted he be given the
chance. If he won, the money would make it all worth it, he
said, and so the fight went ahead.

Unfortunately for Ley his dreams of winning went with him when Hamed dropped him with some heavy blows. Tony saw his eyes glaze over, and as soon as the first bell went he was more than ready with some advice.

If he knocks you down again make sure you look at me.

Round 2 saw Alan go down again, and by the time the ref got to four or five Ley's eyes finally found Tony's who then promptly stopped the fight.

The first and only time Megan's boy has ever had to do this, but he knew the score and as disappointing as it was, he wasn't prepared to watch this young brave-heart get battered for nothing.

Life continued to prove interesting both inside the ring and out, but there was more to come of the latter that would draw him in another direction. Having kept his hand in occasional security work, a chance meeting one day in a pub saw Tony join forces with a fellow door-man called Kevin Boshier.

The year was 1993, the setting, a lively pub that's still going called The Dodger in Newport. The Landlady had called Kevin downstairs to deal with three unruly customers.

The trio were not happy when they were asked to leave and resisted all efforts to do so quietly. As the tension mounted, Tony, who had been enjoying a quiet drink, watched as the situation unfolded. He'd never met Boshier before, but they'd seen each other about town and now as the situation swiftly escalated he found he couldn't sit back and jumped into the fray.

He went for the biggest one and knocked him clean out with a knock on the chin. By this time Boshier had got the other guy outside where Tony, still fired up, put the other one down.

The Landlady was thrilled and Boshier had made a new friend. It was agreed they were a winning team and they decided to join forces.

Local pubs were crying out for good security and both Tony and Kevin were only too happy to oblige. Soon they had a solid crew up and running that took care of most of Newport and the surrounding areas.

For the next few years Tony coached by day as he tried to stop fights at night, and as the business steadily grew deep inside he knew it wasn't enough.

Kevin recalls this as being a particularly tough time for Tony. The security business was flourishing, but things in the coaching department were not.

Despite his best efforts administering to the dreams of budding young fighters, Tony found himself being let down time and time again. Having relinquished his own desire to attain global recognition in the world of boxing, he'd sought instead, to bring his skills to the ring as a coach, but success was proving to be elusive.

There were also issues in his personal life and these were beginning to reach a head.

Relations between him and his partner had been contentious for a number of years, and he freely admits that he was not the faithful kind during the years they were together. The steady stream of women who patronised the nightclubs he worked meant he often gave way to temptation, and emotions, especially when he didn't return home at the end of the night, ran high and understandably so.

Eventually he moved out from the family home but not before another two daughters had come along and another son by a different mother.

Despite Tony's propensity for playing the field, family ties however, have always been very important to him. After his mother passed away he discovered various relatives living in Malta who he remains in regular contact with to this day.

Fortunately, another favourite relative, Ann Noyes, isn't so far away down in Penarth. They meet up as often as they can and like all family members she is extremely proud of his achievements - but not, as Tony often reminds her, as much as his mother would be. He attributes all of his success to Megan and her early influence and together they cherish her memory.

Friendships have also played a very large part in his life and he has forged a particularly strong bond with ex-scaffolder Allen Freeman. Born and bred in Newport this special man has been regarded by Tony for over thirty years as the father he never had. Allen, in turn, looks on Tony as a son and the closeness is evident when you speak to them.

Like any proud parent, Allen takes pleasure in Tony's achievements and how far he's come, not just as an individual, but as a loving father who always did the best for his children.

Theirs is a special relationship, and although Allen is pretty much house-bound following a work-related accident, Tony continues to visit the man he calls dad every day.

Loyalty has ever been one of Tony's strongest characteristics, as is an extremely lively sense of humour. Should you find yourself deep within the inner sanctum of friendship then know that nobody is spared; including Allen, who jumped into his nice, new bed one night only to find himself crashing through to the floor after Tony had removed the bolts!

No one is exempt from this wicked sense of humour. Even family members can find themselves the recipient of strange phone-calls informing them of bogus accidents and the need to take out insurance!

This penchant for fun and games has no doubt been inherited from his grandfather, an inveterate tease whose favourite was to spike the children's sweets with chilli-powder.

Tony may have met his match, however, when he struck up a

friendship with Kevin Kavanagh, now the owner of C & E Travel. The two first met when Kevin drove taxi's before working for Tony briefly on the doors about town. They enjoyed each other's sense of humour to the point they regularly tried to out-prank each other and in ways that would test the firmest of friendships.

An example of this was when they were travelling back to Newport after a night out in Cardiff and Tony, as is his wont, had fallen asleep. He had recently finished a liaison with a certain young lady, and Kevin decided to facilitate a 'reunion' on Tony's behalf.

As Megan's boy snoozed on the back seat of the taxi, Kevin got busy with his phone and began texting this poor unsuspecting woman with words of remorse and unrequited love.

He was on his way to her house - would he be assured of a welcome?

The response was warm and full of delight. Yes, of course! She'd even put the kettle on!

As promised Megan's boy was duly delivered and unceremoniously dumped on the stairs, still oblivious and still fast asleep.

When he woke the next morning, it was to find himself in a very embarrassing situation with the realisation his friend had played an absolute blinder!

Just to add to his misfortune, Kevin had also removed Tony's crutches leaving him to hop with barely a scrap of dignity out of the house to a waiting taxi!

Relieving Tony of his crutches was a particular favourite of this particular friend - throwing them out of a moving taxi onto the M4 being the most memorable!

Tony's leg was to prove troublesome for many years after the car incident. Despite the pins holding it together there was a permanent weakness that would see the leg suddenly snap without warning. But the show, as they say, always went on and during this period Tony was back and fore between Cardiff and Newport as the security business took off.

He also did a stint in Chepstow's only nightclub that was memorable for the fact his leg snapped again during an altercation, but typically Tony was more concerned about losing his shoe! Another operation saw him back on the crutches, but he still had to earn a living and so you'd find him propped on a stool just inside the door as his counterparts manned the entrance. He remained averse to claiming any kind of state benefit and would hobble from job to job, still very much in control of the business and driven by a strong sense of pride.

Downtime would be taken abroad where he'd enjoy sun-filled shenanigans with friends and partners, Cyprus being most memorable when he stepped out of the pool and his leg snapped again. Remarkably this weakness seems to have resolved itself since then and he's not had any further problems for several years. Trouble, however, always seemed to follow him, and there was one incident he was involved in when he wasn't working on the door.

He'd gone out with his partner and another couple to a regular haunt in town. As usual it was jam-packed at the bar, and if you didn't have a glass in your hand you'd be assured of a very long wait!

Tony felt someone grab at his glass and there then ensued a tussle with some random stranger who, despite all reasoning, refused to let go.

After a couple of minutes of this most bizarre game of tug of war Megan's boy had had enough.

'Have it!' he said and let go.

Before he knew what was happening the stranger smashed the glass across his head and in that moment Tony can recall the horrified recoil as the bar-staff were liberally sprayed with his blood.

The blow had slashed open a main artery but the shock of the assault only lasted a milli-second before Tony took him down to the floor as people screamed and shouted all around them.

It was a shocking turn of events, and as the duo grappled on the floor Tony's blood was everywhere including all over his hapless assailant who was now getting a pounding beneath the furious fists of Megan's boy. When the police turned up they assumed that he was the aggressor and that the blood was that of his victim before closing the club.

The doormen, seeking to defuse the situation shoved the perp out of a fire door but as the truth emerged about what had actually happened, Tony's assailant was long gone.

After having his wound attended to, which took several stitches, Megan's boy simmered with the need to have justice, but no one was talking until sometime later a connection was made by sheer chance.

Armed with this new information Tony went to the police and his attacker soon found himself in an Identity Parade.

The rest, as they say, is history – or so Tony thought – when justice was served to his assailant to the tune of an 18 month sentence and everyone involved moved on.

Everyone seemingly except for the attacker who, no sooner after serving his sentence, came looking for revenge.

Coming across three punters one day propping up the wrong end of the bar, Megan's boy asked them to move. They were blocking the point of exit for the bar-staff and it soon became apparent that they were doing so deliberately.

As one of the trio became abusive they were told in no uncertain terms to get out. Tony couldn't understand what their problem was, but that too soon became apparent when the main instigator told him to meet him in the car park outside.

Initially Megan's boy demurred. He was at work. There was no reason to go outside and fight just because an evicted customer demanded it. This character, however, was persistent and so finally persuaded, Tony duly went into the car park and knocked his tormentor out!

Shortly afterwards the police turned up and made a beeline for Tony. They had received a complaint, they said, about an assault. As they reeled off the allegation Megan's boy listened in growing disbelief.

It was a fair fight, he said, and at the insistence of the complainant who, along with his two friends had been thrown out of the club because they were obviously looking for trouble.

He asked for the name of the aggrieved party and upon hearing who it was the penny dropped!

Tony hadn't recognised the face – it had been eighteen months after all – but he remembered the name.

Once the Police were furnished with the details they went away, and the charge was dropped. But Megan's boy still marvels to this day that the assailant who attacked *him* should see fit to dispense revenge for something that *he* had done!

Despite all of the distractions however, he never lost his love for boxing and carried on coaching, crutches or not, as he dreamed of better days ahead.

.

ROUND 7 THE GYM

Ex-steel worker Roger Williams is head coach and the
longest-serving trainer at St. Joe's and is as dedicated as
Tony to the continued success of this previously little-known
gym.

St. Joseph's ABC was started by four local men Charlie
Byron, Mike Holland, Bernard Hurley and Royston
Chambers back in the 70's. The building, which had once
operated as a snooker hall, was tatty and badly in need of
repair, but passion kept the doors open with a steady trickle
of would-be champs and local youngsters.

St. Joe's is where it all truly began for Megan's boy, and as
you'd expect it is officially his second home, although some
may argue it's his first! It's a busy gym where it is unusual
to find quiet moments. If there isn't a film crew in
attendance, there are wandering photographers, visiting
reporters, private training sessions, and the ever-steady
stream of seasoned fighters and wide-eyed amateurs.

The place buzzes with barely-suppressed energy and has a
friendly atmosphere that envelops you as soon as you walk
in. Security cameras watch every move as proud parents
mingle with professionals and the rising smell of sweat

permeates the very air amidst the thuds and grunts and murmuring voices.

It also has no shortage of colourful characters and you need look no further than the principle trainers for that! Banter is the by-word and never a crossed one between any of them in over 20 years. No mean feat in an environment that cultivates competitiveness and it's fair to say they are each and every one of them extremely proud of that, and quite rightly so.

Roger Williams has always been in the fighting game and taught Martial Arts before a fracas in the street with, of all people, 'Sammy' Sims, saw him change direction. In fact he'd rumbled with Sims more than once out and about in town, and it was after these encounters that he realised he wanted to learn how to fight - but with the gloves on! Despite these initial hostilities between them, Roger and Sims became good friends and soon the former was a regular visitor to the gym as he then became Sammy's trainer. He also had his moment in the ring. A bout with a seasoned boxer called Ian Winslet, who, Roger, to his delighted surprise, soundly defeated. His one and only fight, and having tasted victory and had the experience, he was happy to walk away and concentrate on the coaching.

Life has a funny way of pulling people together and little did Roger know all those years ago when he first clocked Tony that he would also become *his* trainer for his last couple of fights! Such is the carousel of boxing that he should then find himself training alongside him when Megan's boy stepped down from the ring for the last time.

Their association began in earnest and together they coached both the amateurs and the professionals before legislation by the W.A.B.A (Welsh Amateur Boxing Association) made this very difficult. Whereas once St. Joseph's gym had four trainers for all boxers they now divided accordingly. Roger and Megan's boy initially took on the professionals, with the other coaches Billy Reynolds and Dave Exon taking care of the amateurs.

Billy Reynolds is Tony's Corner Man No.3 and like Roger started out in Martial Arts. By day he's a lecturer at Cardiff Vale College, and despite a busy workload, rarely misses a fight. He's quite a presence in the gym as he is in the ring. A shrewd straight-shooter, talkative, informative and with a lively sense of humour!
Having worked the corners from the mighty to the mundane his regular stints give great insight into what actually goes on at the end of each bout. When a boxer returns to the corner it is never to raised voices and only one that they will hear. Tony is the focus, the oasis, the port in the storm amidst the din and the adrenaline, his style is tailor-made to each boxer and this comes across, even on camera.

Dave 'Dai' Exton takes care of the amateurs and arranges all of their bouts. He is a solid fatherly presence in the gym and along with Tony he is currently coaching another promising young individual Ben Wetter, British Schoolboy Champ and the first to win a Silver medal.
He has seen many young fighters come and go, the most memorable being Damien Dunnion. All four coaches were in agreement this young bantamweight had potential as he went on to become Welsh and British Schoolboy Champion.
Encouraged by his winning streak Dunnion duly turned pro, and despite losing his debut in July 2001 a chance to show his mettle came just three months later.
Tony received a call from ex-boxer and renowned coach Dai Gardiner with the offer of a fight. The opponent was a young Mongolian bantamweight by the name of Shinny Bayaar.

He'd been brought over at no small expense, and despite a slight discrepancy in weight Tony finally agreed to the match. On the appointed date as the two came together in the ring, Dunnion well and truly did the business much to the shock of all who had backed his opponent.

Words were exchanged afterwards between Tony and those concerned, and although the Welsh win caused a few ripples it went some way in putting St. Joseph's on the map. Unfortunately Dunnion never fought again, but Bayaar, who came over with another Mongolian, Choi Tseveenpurev. Bayaar went on to win the British Flyweight title several years later with Tseveenpurev taking the WBF World Featherweight title in April 2004.

Dunnion's achievement, however, had given hope and was a glimmer of the success yet to come.

If the walls of St. Joseph's could talk I'm sure they'd have a few stories to tell. But in the absence of this much wished for phenomena, the walls reverberate in a different way deep within the lower regions.

In the basement you'll find not one, but two recording studios. One is Pentalk Lab Music Services, the baby of Jamie Winchester, whose musical connections read like a dream! Access is usually via the gym and many a hapless visitor has been stopped by Tony who demands they put some gloves on first and do a few rounds. In response to the inevitable confusion he will then beetle his brow and demand, 'This is a boxing gym! Does it look like a recording studio to you? If you come in here, you have to fight!' To which the poor musician will visibly wilt before desperately looking towards the door.

Such is the wit of Megan's boy. Sometimes he just can't help himself!

Visitors come to St. Joe's for various reasons and it's not all strictly boxing.

Take Matt Hookings, for instance, Newport-born actor and founder of Camelot films. Matt was researching boxing techniques for his upcoming film *Prizefighter* and came by the gym for advice. Tony was only too happy to help, but recommended Matt actually put on the gloves and get into the ring, because there are some things that simply can't be explained – you have to experience them and boxing is one of them.

Prizefighter tells the story of a talented young boxer (played by Matt) who became the youngest champ ever at the turn of the 19th Century. It is a poignant tale not least because it is based upon a true story. The film starts production in April 2019.

Matt has been training with Tony now for two years and has watched 146 boxing films as part of his research but none have been more rewarding than stepping in the ring itself, which he thanks Tony for.

In the meantime Camelot films have just released *Winter Ridge* that has already been scooping up awards and rave reviews. *Winter Ridge* hits cinemas next month including Newport.

Another individual to reap the benefit of Tony's expertise is local businesswoman Jodie Emes who runs The Greenhouse pub in Cwmbran. Jodie has managed a few less than savoury establishments in her time and after a particularly hair-raising encounter with some drunks decided she needed to invest in some self-defence. For the past few years she's trained under the tutelage of Megan's boy and her skills now are such that she enjoys the training immensely and packs quite a punch!

The gym has also had the odd celebrity pass through its doors. Take Alesha Dixon, for instance, who came to interview Super bantamweight Robbie Turley, who also happens to possess a fine singing voice! When Turley isn't slugging it out in the gym, he can sometimes be found otherwise engaged in the musical scene. Having performed at the Jools Holland Jam club in London, Rob has also recorded a number in the Deco studios with none other than the Jamiroqui Jam band. Super bantamweight or Singing Superstar? Who knows - only that Robbie Turley will be giving both his best shot in the coming months, so his name is definitely one you might want to keep an ear out for in the future.

St Joseph's is nothing but forthcoming in its dealings with both the outside world and within. It is indicative of the whole gym ethos that all sides work together as they share pads and bags. There is also much kindness amidst the slog and the sweat when kit, beyond the realms of many a poor amateur, will find its way on to grateful hands and thankful feet, courtesy of 'the management' and this they do gladly. The boxing world has ever looked after its own – and beyond in the form of charitable events and St. Joe's is no exception.

Photographs, signed gloves, special appearances. Ask, and Megan's boy will do his best to deliver. Having come from nothing Tony understands the gift of giving and believes it takes nothing away to give something of yourself even if it's a few minutes, and he passes this philosophy on to his boxers.

One particular instance was when the Garrett family came down to the gym from Wrexham in North Wales – a journey of well over 3 hours! Their son, Cian, who was eight at the time, was a big fan of boxing and desperate to meet his hero,

Lee Selby.

The gym-visit was also to be Cian's Christmas present and so Tony, once he realised how far they'd travelled, pulled out all the stops determined to make their visit memorable. After the requisite tour of the gym and photos with both Lee and Gary Buckland - came the bonus and every little boy's dream who loved boxing. A sparring session with a World Champion! And as Selby donned the gloves he offered confidence and a fiver to Cian if he could punch him on the chin - which of course he did!

Another time Tony revisited his past with a visit to old school pal and dancer-in-crime Martyn Fowler at the Rugby Academy in Cardiff. Martyn is the Director of Rugby and a Level 4 instructor at the Cardiff and Vale College and had invited Tony in for a talk. This he duly did along with Lee Selby who enthralled their audience further with a demo on the pads!

As a trainer Tony draws no regular wage and so sponsorship is vital in the overall set-up of the gym Payday is fight-day and coaches get the standard 10%. By his own admittance it is a tenuous way of earning a living, and he counts his blessings regularly in the guise of local businesswoman, Sharyn Donnachie who sponsors the gym.

Sharyn, shrewd business woman and co-owner of Cardiff's Capital Cabs grew up watching boxing and counts Former light welterweight / welterweight Champion Ricky Hatton as a particular favourite.

She's shown great support for St. Joe's and its fighters over the years, holding Tony and the rest of the team in the highest regard for no other merit than their dedication. Having experienced first-hand the benefits of personal training at St Joe's, Sharyn appreciates the hard work that goes in and often for little or no payment.

Patrick Killian, international and roving artist pops by occasionally and is also the epitome of 'local boy does good'. From a village in the Swansea Valley Patrick first met Tony some 15 years ago when he was boxing at Cwmcarn ABC. Patrick was just a teenager then but Tony remembers him as a good fighter who punched well.
Little did either of them know at that time where their paths would take them, and Tony recalls bumping into Patrick in the lobby at the MGM Grand in Las Vegas, a far cry from the sweat-filled rings of the South Wales Valleys, and how they'd expressed their mutual respect at how far the other had come. Patrick continues to live a busy life as boxing portraiture takes him world-wide and is also Ambassador to the Amelia Mae Foundation.

You cross paths will all kinds of people at the gym and Newport-born photographer Sarah Hopkins and her husband have become something of a regular fixture. Tony particularly likes her style of capturing off-key moments and has since kept her and her photographic skills extremely busy! Besides covering the wedding earlier this year, her work now adorns the entire ceiling of the upstairs gym.
A big fan of boxing Sarah is no stranger to combat having recently beaten off cancer and her choice of imagery certainly reflects a steely grit. It is a striking collage of boxers, past and present captured in action forever. A tribute and testament to all the blood sweat and *sheer* hard work that goes into becoming a champion.

St. Joseph's, never a dull moment and always a hot-bed of *something* going on! No one is allowed to pull rank here, whether you are World class or not. Megan's boy has made it his business to cultivate a strong sense of equality where everyone is treated the same and it clearly works. Title-holders and young bright-eyed boxers of the future work out next to each other as proud parents look on and dreams hang heavy in the air. It is a good place – but oh, if only if those walls   could   talk!

ROUND 8 BLOOD, SWEAT AND SUCCESS

In 2006 Tony went out to Australia for the Commonwealth
Games as coach to amateur boxers, Matthew Edmunds and
Mohammed Nasir – both of whom won their bouts. Prior to
the visit he had arranged to meet with Boxing Promoter,
Chris Sanigar, and suggested they hook up for future events.
Tony had the boxers but opportunities to showcase them
locally were thin on the ground. Sanigar, a fellow boxer
back in the day agreed and it was to be the start of a winning
combination.

They staged their first show at Newport Centre on 15th
September 2006. It proved to be a great success with all four
boxers winning their fights – Gary Buckland, Matthew
Edmunds, Jamie Way and Robbie James respectively.

Gary Buckland was of particular interest. Hailing from a
Welsh Romany family in Cardiff, he'd arrived at St Joe's in
early 2000 after becoming somewhat disillusioned whilst
training at another gym. His father had asked around and it
was suggested he check out St Joseph's. This he duly did,
and it wasn't long before Megan's boy knew he had a
champion on his hands.

Naturally blessed with a 'boxing brain', Gary's style of
combat was as courageous as it was versatile, and he soon

made it clear he wasn't interested in trophies and titles – he was in it for the money and the fight.

Tony approached local manager Brian Powell and suggested he sign Buckland up. Powell, who had worked Joe Calzaghe's corner back in the day, saw him in action and was suitably impressed.

It was a foregone conclusion and in 2004 Buckland turned Professional.

His debut came on 5th March 2005 with a four-round bout against Warren Dunkley in Dagenham, who he defeated on points, much to the displeasure of the promoters who'd been banking on their boy.

It was a promising start and Gary didn't disappoint as he went on to comfortably win his next three fights.

Tony looks back on these years with fond recall as Buckland's rising profile made for some memorable moments, like when they went to Alicante during a very hot July.

The year was 2006, the bout was to take place outside for the first time and the temperature was phenomenal. As Team Borg made their way to the ring Gary's heart dropped when his opponent came into view. Ubadel Soto was swathed in towels despite the searing heat. This didn't bode well. If his opponent could stand the heat *and* be wrapped up like that – then what chance did he have!

So imagine Buckland's surprise when he emerged victorious – which made winning all the sweeter despite the sweat!

A couple of years later in March 2008, the team went up to Nottingham for what was going to be an indelible display on Buckland's behalf when faced with the 'Pitbull'.

Alex 'the Pitbull' Spliko was from Latvia and like a giant compared to Buckland. As they waited for the first bell Gary eyed him from the corner and reckoned he'd met more than his match.

Despite the three and a half extra inches, however, Buckland more than rose to the challenge and knocked the 'giant' out with a three-punch combination. It was an incredible moment but no one was more surprised than the 'Dynamo'!

It was an impressive beginning as Buckland swept all before him as he steadily boxed his way forward until he had his first defeat, when he lost on points to Ben Murphy in Portsmouth 2008.

But his unbroken record over the preceding four years had not gone unnoticed and the media had soon turned their attention to this raw Welsh talent coming out of St Joe's. Buckland re-emerged in grand style winning his next four fights before missing out on both the British and European title to John Murray in February 2010.

At his next bout in York Hall, Bethnal Green, in light of his recent defeat, Tony had impressed on him the need to 'shine', and Buckland, ever obedient to his trainer, had liberally covered himself with Vaseline before going on to win his bout!

He was back on top of his game and nothing demonstrated this more than in November later that year when he dropped to Super featherweight. Sky Sports were hosting their professional boxing tournament, *Prizefighter*, and Buckland decided to throw in his lot.

After a gruelling and dogged display, he walked away with the £32,000 prize-fund – a huge amount of money and a massive achievement!

No one could deny Buckland was the business - his feat putting both his profile and St Joe's on the map with Sky Sports and the ensuing press attention.

Megan's boy worked the corner on all of his 38 fights and only ever had to take Buckland to task once. This was after the first round in the Prize-fighting competition, when Tony told him in no uncertain terms that if he boxed in the second as he had in the first, then basically they could forget it. His words hit the mark and the rest, as they say, is history.

Both he and Tony have enjoyed a father/son relationship since Gary first came to St Joe's at 14 years of age. But all relationships have their weak spots and on the night before Buckland's first fight as a professional one thing became apparent – Megan's boy could snore – loudly!
Unable to stand the din anymore and desperate for sleep before his big night, Gary slipped from the room and went off to find ear-plugs. It was the first and the last time they would share a room together. Indeed, it's fair to say that no one will share a room with Megan's boy when the team are away! He can snore for Wales apparently and then some!
The remainder of his career saw Buckland leave an unforgettable trail of wins, losses and knock-outs, his most memorable against Gary Sykes before hanging up the gloves in 2016. It had been a glittering, and at times controversial career that saw him take the Welsh, Celtic and British title, until the passion that had always driven him began to lose its edge.
In his own words it is "The hunger that wins on the night" and he had taken his fill.

Gary's younger brother Mitchell also proved he has what it takes to take him to the top when he turned professional in 2012. At lightweight he hit the ring in fine style, becoming Celtic boxing champion and with all the flair of his brother. Mitch has since moved to another gym since this project started, but both he and Gary remain memorable for the many grudge-fights they had, and it is with humour that Tony recalls the first time it happened.

He'd got a frantic call from Roger: *The Buckland brothers had fallen out and were slugging it out old-style in the ring. He needed to get down to the gym and fast!*

This Tony duly did, only to find them going at it hammer and tongs minus the usual protection of gum-shields and headguards. There was a real risk of either one getting hurt – not the best prospect for two of his best fighters! But Tony, realising that this was how they settled their differences, reached a compromise. In case of future disputes of this nature, (and there were some) he would be happy to go with the 'blows' on the proviso he was there to referee, and they wore their guards.

You'll still find Gary at the gym most nights training with his boy. Like a lot of boxers who spent much of their formative years at the gym, he still enjoys the ethos that makes St Joe's so unique. He looks back on his fighting career with a mixture of pride and nostalgia; his manner is both modest and philosophical, as he readily admits that if he had his time again he would do things differently. Enjoying the odd drink between tournaments and training was, he feels now, an ill-formed choice fuelled by the complacency of youth. He doesn't dwell on it, but he reflects with the wisdom of an older head as the warning words of his manager still echo.

But Buckland's rise to prominence didn't come alone, as a young featherweight from Barry whose prowess in the ring soon marked him out as a serious contender and like a strike of Fate both picked up a world title within months of each other prompting the headline:

'It took Tony Borg 10 years to become an overnight sensation'

As Selby picked up the British and Commonwealth titles
with Buckland winning the British Super Featherweight title
a week later!
Understandably, Tony was very proud of this and after years
of hard slog, his faith in himself and his fighters was finally
starting to pay off.

Selby had come on to the scene as something of an enigma.
There were a few who doubted he'd last the course, but
Megan's boy knew differently and had him firmly in his eye.
On 12th July 2008, Selby had his debut fight at the Newport
Leisure Centre when he defeated Sid Razak. He went on to
win his next three fights – his loss to Samir Mouneimne in
May 2009, proving to be just a blip as Selby proved he was
just warming up.
Then 30th October 2010 saw him knock Dai Davies out in
the second round and claim the BBBofC Area Welsh Title.
The following year he was back in Newport on 30th July
when he took on James Ancliffe for the vacant Celtic
Featherweight title. A stoppage in the eighth round saw
Selby once more victorious, as he then cast his eyes for what
would be his biggest challenge yet.

The British and Commonwealth Featherweight title was then
held by Stephen 'Swifty' Smith. With 12 wins under his belt
he was undoubtedly a force to be reckoned with, but he
wasn't swift enough to get away from a left hand by
'Lightning', and on 17th September 2011, Selby walked
away the new champion like a man walking on air!
It was the fulfilment of a long-held dream and an incredible
achievement. Selby was on fire! As he set his sights on
winning the World title, he systematically steamed through
every opponent set against him – most notably undefeated
Corey McConnell from Australia in April 2013.

McConnell's team threw the towel in at the fifth as 'Lightning' did the business.

Tony describes this time as a whirlwind of excitement and attention, as Selby blazed a trail taking Welsh, Celtic, British and Commonwealth titles, but the best was yet to come and for Lee it couldn't come fast enough.

His chance finally came in Hull on 13th July 2013 when he stepped into the ring with Romanian title-holder, Viorel Simion. Undefeated, and ranked by WBC as fourth in the world, Simion was a tough opponent but Selby gave it everything he had and came away victorious.

2014 dawned and the EBU European Featherweight title was wanting. On 1st February Lee went up against Rendall Munroe at the Motorpoint Arena in Cardiff and added it to his already impressive array of titles.

Next up was the IBF and this title was to be the pinnacle of his boxing career. The date was 30th May 2015 and the venue the prestigious O2 in London. The title holder was Evgeny Gradovich, a Russian-born boxer who lived in the States and was trained by Mexicans. He was also a quality fighter and commanded much respect.

As soon as Lee stepped into the ring he unleashed the 'lightning' and outclassed and out-boxed his opponent leading to a TKO that saw Selby the new World Champion. It was an incredible moment that every young boxer dreams of.

Selby went on to successfully defend his IBF title four more times; the fourth against Barras at Wembley. This was to be his bravest and most memorable performance, having learned just hours before about the passing of his mother. The date was 15th July 2017, a date that would remain inscribed forever.

Despite entreaties from his team and family to withdraw from the fight, Lee refused. He showed his true mettle that night with a blistering performance as the boxing world looked on with maximum respect.

Just a few months later he saw off challenger Eduardo Ramirez in London, little knowing that his next fight in Leeds would mark the end of his reign as IBF World Champion and there we will revisit in the last but not final round.

Selby and Buckland, without doubt were the winning formula that raised the profile of St Joseph's - not to mention the coaching skills of Megan's boy. But there have also been others who have thrived at the hands of Borg Boxing.

Andrew Selby, younger brother to Lee, has a skill-set most boxers can only dream of and has recently come back with a vengeance. He is currently the British Flyweight Champion and has his eyes fixed firmly on a World title. Keen to put the past behind him, he has been training hard in readiness to go back to doing what he does best. Rated number one in the boxing world, he is, to quote Tony, "The most outstanding natural fighter I have ever known" and when you see him in action you can see why.

He rose through the amateurs like a rocket before going on to win his six fights during the World Series Boxing in 2012-13, under the 'British Lionhearts' banner.

2014 saw him go for gold in the Commonwealth Games in the flyweight division, but his gum shield kept coming out and that cost him the match.

With such an impressive record and rated as best amateur in the world, Andrew turned professional in 2015 and swiftly showed everyone that he was the business.

His debut on 30th October saw him stop his opponent Haji Juma just two minutes into the fourth round, and he has since blazed a trail with a further nine wins and no defeats, earning him the alias 'Superstar'.

That he has something special, there is no doubt.

Megan's boy, who waits for no man, never mind a flighty fighter, has ever kept the faith with this fine young flyweight – and notwithstanding, Andrew is thankful for Tony's support.

May their association ever stay strong and Andrew fulfill his ambition that will take him to the top!

Light-middleweight, Fred Evans, another Welsh Romany from Cardiff, appeared in the gym in about 2005, having boxed steadily since he was 10 years old. His potential was evident at an early age when he won a gold medal in 2007 at the World Championships in Hungary. He followed this up with another gold for Wales four years later at the European Amateur Boxing Championships in Ankara.

He was on a roll, and in the same year emerged from the 2011 World Amateur Boxing Championships in Azerbaijan to become the first Welsh boxer to qualify for the 2012 Olympics. An amazing achievement with the promise of much more to come. Since his debut as a professional in May last year, Evans remains undefeated and is as hungry as they come!

Another boxer from the South Wales Valleys who has gone from strength to strength is Gavin Gwynne. A rangy lightweight, to-date unbeaten, he, too, has thrived beneath the tough tutelage of Tony's expertise, and is now reaping the rewards as the sponsorship deals roll in, courtesy of boxing enthusiast Phil Whaley of Team GG.

Gavin, like all of Tony's fighters, has gained immeasurably

in confidence and seen his skills improve since making his debut in July 2016. He currently stands undefeated with nine wins under his belt and a deep-seated assurance he can go all the way.

Fellow lightweight Lance Cooksey is also showing much promise with 7 solid wins since his first professional fight in May 2017. Interestingly, his father, who shares the same first name, goes way back with Tony when they boxed the same amateur circuit during the years of 1979-1981. Having known Megan's boy back in his hey-day and with no other coach in mind, he brought Lance to meet Tony and has since had the satisfaction of seeing his son thrive under his tutelage.

Daniel Barton, is St. Joe's middleweight with movie-star looks has shown himself to be a good prospect with three wins and a draw since making his debut in April last year. Having boxed all over the world as an amateur, Barton is keenly committed and also one to watch.

Robbie Vernon, who enjoyed a promising amateur career threw in the towel for some years before recently making a come-back as Light-welterweight and is the latest new pro on the block. His style is quite feisty and already he has gained a good following.

Jamie Cox who has 27 bouts under his belt with just two defeats has also recently come on board, and having held the Commonwealth Light/middleweight title from 2011 to 2012 has already shown tremendous potential.

Yet amidst this plethora of titanic male energy and surging testosterone, came something a bit different for Megan's boy and he hasn't looked back since: Women's boxing!

He had known and trained a couple of females who fought in Martial Arts, indeed, as far back as 1994 he had taught Tai Kwon Do World Champion, Newport's Pam Glover how to punch!

Pam recalls how difficult it was to get past the door of any boxing gym in those days. Women working out in gyms just didn't happen, so she struck gold with Tony, because not only did he allow her into the hallowed ring, he also coached her for nothing! Sheer testament to his generosity of spirit when helping a 'damsel in distress', as I'm sure you'll agree!

It was some years later before he actually came across women boxing. In November 2013, he flew out to Germany with Frank Maloney and Commonwealth Gold Medallist Jamie Arthur. At the weigh-in there were two women and Tony was, by his own admittance, quietly horrified. The fact that they were also both very attractive only added to his angst.

He never thought he'd actually see women thrashing it out in a boxing ring, *never mind his own gym!*

Yet there are accounts of women going toe-to-toe since the 18thcentury, and a demonstration of female fighters at the Olympic Games in 1904 was just a taste of things to come. Boxing between women had always been controversial, but in 1988 Sweden surprised everyone when their Amateur Boxing Association decided to lift the ban. This then saw their British counterpart follow suit nine years later in 1997 when they sanctioned the first female amateur fight.

This feminine foray into the ring of '*All* Man's Land', however, was not received well by everyone and the British Boxing Board of Control refused to have anything to do with it. But they reckoned without the 'Fleetwood Assassin', better known as Jane Crouch (MBE), who not only challenged them but took them to court – and won – becoming the first British female boxer to be issued a license in 1998.

It was an incredible achievement and a wake-up call to the Boxing world; women were now allowed on the canvas *by law* and they wanted to fight!
Tony had personal experience of this and of the *Fleetwood Assassin* when she came by St Joseph's one day looking to spar.
Despite her best efforts to persuade him, however, Tony declined her offer unable or unwilling to raise his gloves to a woman for fear of what *could* happen once the competitive spirit in both of them kicked in.
But the writing was on the wall, and having accepted the rules for Women's Boxing, The IBA (amateur) approved the European Cup with the endorsement of the first World Championship following on two years later. But it wasn't until 2012 that the Olympics parted the ropes after a landmark decision in 2009, and the scene, as they say, was set.

As Megan's boy absorbed these new changes he also began to take an interest in the fighting skills of the 'fairer sex' and his first opportunity came in the form of a local policewoman, Jess Jones. Her skills in the ring he freely admits, showed more than potential and this bore fruit when she went on to win a title at the British Championships.
Next up was Rachael Buckland *née* Pritchard from Magor. Small, fair and feisty, Rachael soon showed her mettle becoming Welsh champion at bantamweight before an unfortunate accident put paid to a promising career.
Yet her achievement had demonstrated clearly to Megan's

boy that women were not just capable of putting on the gloves, but that they were also able to put up a good fight. By the time Ashley Brace came along he was practically converted. Ashley first came to his attention at the weigh-in for her debut fight back in 2015.

She was no stranger to the ring, having started kick-boxing at six years of age, before developing an interest in boxing by her mid-teens, blown away by the skills of Ricky Hatton! So, when Ashley's father, who was her principle trainer, called Tony one day, it marked the beginning of what was to become an exciting journey for both trainer and his newly-acquired 'Storm'!

And storm she did, through her next few fights, as Tony's style of coaching paid off as did Ashley's sparring sessions with the likes of Selby and Buckland. Like all of the boxers in St Joe's, she enjoys the vibe and is fully accepted into the fighting fraternity, but it is with Megan's boy whom she shares the closest connection.

He has nurtured and brought out the best in her, spurring her on, improving her jab, perfecting her in the art of employing 'the poker face' when hefty body-shots have tried to dictate otherwise.

By Ashley's own admittance he has calmed the 'storm' redirecting her energies into a formidable, more controlled force of nature, and this was demonstrated clearly on 14th April 2018 in Cardiff when she took the EBU European Female Super Flyweight title.

A first for a British female boxer and a massive achievement for Ashley who slept with the belt for a week afterwards! But she had gone into the ring that night with a determination to win – not just for herself, but for Tony and the rest of the team who have embraced her dream with the same dedication. Thanks to their faith in her and that of her trainer, Ashley proudly bears the titles of Bantamweight WBC International Champion and Super Flyweight European Champion.

This 'quirky individual' as Tony fondly refers to her, will be one to watch as she embarks on the next stage of her fighting career, safe in the knowledge that Megan's boy has got her back.

ROUND 9 BOXING IS THE GAME

St Joseph's has seen many aspiring boxers pass through its doors over the years. Some stay, some go – but that also is the nature of the game. Professionals such as Joe Cordina, Sean Mcgoldrick, Craig Evans and Morgan Jones all enjoyed unbeaten success under the tutelage of Megan's boy before they moved on. But Tony can take pride in their achievements during the time they were with him with titles that included British, European and Commonwealth gold.

His contribution to boxing was recognised in 2011 when he was awarded 'Welsh Coach of the Year' – a well-deserved accolade that he picked up for the second time this year. (2018)

But the jewel in St Joseph's crown has undoubtedly been Lee Selby.

Like Megan's boy, Lee's beginnings are humble. Family tradition has it that Mr. Selby (even more senior than the present one, being his great, great grandfather) originally came from Ireland in a horse and cart before settling in South Wales. Whether this story is true or not, boxing, however, is most definitely in the blood as his father can testify.

Lee Selby Senior is no stranger to boxing, having first took up the gloves in 1977 when ex-RAF boxing champ Henry Brown opened a gym above the old EastEnd Labour Club. A block of flats sits on the site now, but back in the day the gym was a hub of activity as youngsters flocked up its stairs with dreams of fights and fortune.

Lee's father, Peter, was club steward at the time, so whilst he ran the ship downstairs, Selby Senior worked the bags upstairs going on to rack up over 20 bouts with just one defeat.

This was not a bad record and a sign perhaps of the talent we would see –not just in one of his sons, but in two – as both Lee and Andrew Selby went on to take the Welsh boxing world and beyond by storm.

Father and sons are very close and where you'll find one, you'll usually find the other. They share a philosophical view of life whereby nothing is taken for granted. A favourite saying is, *don't assume; makes an ass out of you and me!*

A most fitting adage and an ethos that comes through clearly when you speak to Lee Selby.

For someone who has recently taken a dive from such dizzying heights, there is no self-castigation, no looking back, just maintaining the focus and forging ahead.

You only have to see him in the ring with Tony to see the special rapport that they share. There is an ease between them – an instinctive coming together of energies. Their pad-work is spectacular to witness and second to none!

Lee accords the maximum respect to Tony and vice versa and it is this perhaps, which forms the basis of their success. Ask Tony how he views their working relationship and his response is as complimentary as it is uncompromising: Selby is the epitome of what it takes to become a world champion

– hard-working, disciplined, the consummate professional and the best he's ever trained.

For 'Lightning' the feeling is mutual, and he especially likes the fact that he can always give feedback that is received without offence. Ever-attuned to the needs of each other and still humble enough to take advice, small wonder that theirs has been such a winning combination.

2018 has been a busy year for Megan's boy – what with fights, frights (Emma was extremely late for her wedding!) and of course marital delight when the bride finally said yes! But typical of Tony and his sense of commitment, he was back in the gym the very day after his wedding.

Lee Selby had a bout in Leeds the following Saturday and training time was of the essence. It would be Selby's fifth defence of his IBF title, and what would be his last fight at featherweight.

The honeymoon was postponed as Tony focused on the training, for, as Corner Man No. 3 Billy Reynolds so aptly put it, "He is a boxing man through and through!"

As preparations went on in the Borg camp there was much anticipation surrounding what was rapidly becoming a tournament marked by controversy in the days leading up. Lee's challenger, Warrington, had a big following and the sentiments of some fans were becoming increasingly hostile as the big night loomed. As a precaution all wives, partners and respective family members were told to remain home – Lee Selby Senior, in particular, had actually received death threats so nobody was taking any chances. At the weigh-in Selby was met by a hostile crowd that heckled the Welsh contingent as the boxing world looked on bemused. Contrary to the usual posturing, the mood was decidedly ugly, and by the time Team Borg had returned to their cars they were greeted by a posse and a half-hearted 'attack' as vehicles were kicked and threats issued.

As security did their best to restore order, Team Borg were on their way back to the hotel before they realised that they'd left Tony behind!

Megan's boy, who has faced many challenges in his day and rarely shied from any of them, suddenly found himself in an unenviable position. As the Welsh cavalcade raced away, here he was alone amidst the opposition with 'Borg Boxing' emblazoned across his T-shirt just for good measure!

Bracing himself, he glanced around him and thankfully no attack was imminent as the crowd began to shuffle away, but you can probably imagine what words were said when the car returned to pick him up!

By this time, all everyone wanted was for the match to be done and dusted and to get the hell 'out of Dodge'. It was just another fight, another defence and another victory surely?

Sadly it was not to be.

As one cut followed another Lee was up against it from the first round, and as the blood began to flow the implications of what these injuries meant sent a shiver through the Selby corner.

As the crowd bayed all around them, the team remained calm, the only animated moment being when Chris Sanigar overruled the medic in the fifth to ensure Selby stayed in the fight.

It was a brave and poignant performance as Lee battled on and the team frantically tried to stop the bleeding. Tony knew from the first round that Selby wasn't himself. The months of trying to maintain his weight had obviously taken their toll, and by the time the bell rang out for the twelfth round, it was all over.

The walk back to the changing-room had never seemed so long. Everyone was stunned. Except for Lee, of course because *never assume ...* remember?

As Tony and Billy set off for the long drive back, the mood was strained and at times surreal as they struggled to comprehend what had happened. It was a massive blow to Team Borg and totally unexpected.
The mood going up had been buoyant and confident despite knowing they were going into the 'lion's den', and now as they made their way back down to Wales, Tony's thoughts turned to his imminent honeymoon. He and Emma were due to fly out within hours.
What would his mood be like? Would he be able to enjoy this special time they'd both planned and been waiting for?

It turned out he needn't have worried as the following morning the newly-weds were presented with the most amazing surprise as a Phantom Stretch Rolls Royce drew up to take them to the airport.
It was a memorable and wholly unforeseen start to what was to be an equally memorable and enjoyable few days away.

By the time he returned, Megan's boy looked to the future as Selby issued a statement saying that he would go up a weight and aim for a double world title.
It was just what the good boxing doc had ordered – time to move on, regroup and refocus! Lee may have lost the belt, but Team Borg, having achieved so much to date, are philosophical enough to handle the lows and keep looking to the future – because Lightning has been known to strike twice – right?

And so, what about the man behind the pads who has so captured people's imaginations and who leads such a busy life? What does he do when he's away from the ring? How does he unwind?

Ever sociable, he likes to catch up with friends when time permits, and as father of nine he also has ten grandchildren, (and no stretch marks, if you ask him!) so family life is busy and keeps him on his toes! But when he does want to escape from it all, you'll find him glued in front of the TV watching a good crime drama like the recent hit series, 'Keeping Faith'.

His career has been extraordinary and taken him all over the world. But at heart he remains a home-body, and more than a few days away from the ranch is too long.

When asked of all the destinations he'd visited which one ranked as his favourite, there wasn't a moment's hesitation – London!

Big, busy, bright with everything at your fingertips! What more could you want when away on a fight-night!

He waxed more than lyrical when asked about the least desirable - a trip to Serbia in the summer of 2007.

The usual crew had gone out for the under 19's European Championships and it soon became apparent that there was a problem with the food. Despite the hotel's best efforts, the team just couldn't stomach the copious amount of oil that seemed to accompany everything.

The situation quickly became a culinary stand-off of 'starve or swim' and Team Borg was not up for either.

So off they would trundle, every day, in convoy, in search of something more palatable and infinitely less moist - a far cry from the days when such excursions could only be dreamt of as he starved before a fight!

For Megan's boy the memories of those locust years still reverberate deep within him and you'd think he'd be fussy, or else excessive in regards to his food intake. But he eats normally with no particular likes or dislikes - although red meat has begun to disappear from his diet and he's also not averse to quorn.

For the most part, Tony is relatively easy-going, and it's just as well because you only have to be around him a short time to appreciate just how much attention he receives.
Take the TV crew for instance, who have been in attendance during key family moments and the ease with which he takes it all in his stride. An example of this was seeing Tony being interviewed just an hour before his wedding outside the venue. Half-dressed, with guests arriving all around him, he smiled and nodded as he carried on talking to the camera – the epitome of cool and not a nerve in sight!

The production company were also in attendance during Tony's Stag weekend in Spain, and on this occasion, he was far less relaxed in anticipation of what his friends had planned. As a serial prankster he knew he had it coming and had warned them in advance that *any* interference with *any* part of his anatomy would see them banned from the wedding forthwith.
It wasn't just the fact any shenanigans and inevitable humiliation would be caught on camera that worried him, but once the celebrations were over he would be flying back to yet more cameras at the Ice Arena in Cardiff that night where he had three fighters on the bill!
As the first night got underway all was quiet on the Stag-night front, but Megan's boy wasn't to be lulled into a false sense of security and remained on full alert.
On the second night a taxi drew up outside the club and as soon as Tony caught a glimpse of the passenger he 'legged' it. His vigilant stance paid off – an attempt to handcuff him

to a dwarf for the night had been swiftly thwarted!
As he went to ground in a bar around the corner, his friends, having failed to execute their master-plan, found themselves several hundred pounds lighter and resigned to less controversial entertainment for the remainder of the stay! Suffice to say, Tony could now relax and enjoy his Stag – and despite the frustration of a delayed flight home, he made it to the tournament and with both eyebrows intact!

As to why Megan's boy's exploits are being recorded for posterity, please refer to the section below as kindly provided by the production company.

Little Gem is making a new documentary series with the working title, 'The Family Project'. This will be a unique observational documentary series documenting the lives of four families over the period of 5 years. Each film will tell the story of a single family – its ups and downs; the things that challenge and unite its members; their most difficult times to their happiest moments. It will be an honest, down-to-earth, joyful, uplifting and epic portrait of life in modern Britain told through the prism of an institution most of us belong to, in one form or another – the Family. It is slated to air in 2021.

Despite all of the attention, the kudos and success, however, Tony remains humble and has never forgotten his roots. He often visits Splott and the old haunts of his childhood, sometimes just parking up and soaking up the memories as he appreciates how far he's come.
Emotionally, he is very contained; indeed, he will tell you, and quite openly, that he isn't prone to expressing softer sentiments and will shy away from tears and outbursts. Some years ago, when life wasn't so rosy he teetered on the

edge of depression but refused the offer of medication, deciding in that moment that only he could save himself. Such a strong mentality has been inherited, no doubt, from his mam and grandfather. Both were proud and fiercely independent and it is these qualities that have helped shape him into the man he is today.

He's a natural-born fighter, a survivor and blessed with good *nous* of what makes a good boxer. Lee Selby's success has been proof of that. But then as Megan's boy will tell you, 'The cream always rises to the top' and something tells me the next part of their journey is just beginning...

ROUND 10 GLOVE AND MARRIAGE

There are few things as fickle as fate, and the coming together of Tony and Emma was no exception.

Their paths first crossed in 1998 when Tony's friend, Kevin, offered Emma and her cousin a lift in his taxi. Emma was familiar with Kevin, but she had never seen or heard of Tony before, and seeing a strange dark figure sat in the front of the car, greetings were exchanged but neither thought anything more of it.

Emma had moved away some years before to study 'Business and Languages' at Wolverhampton University and had returned home to Newport unaware of Tony's security ties about town and his association with boxing.

Eventually their paths met and they dated briefly in 1998/99 before things fizzled out. Emma wasn't interested in casual relationships, and Tony, as was his nature at that time, couldn't promise fidelity.

It was to be a few years before their paths crossed again when she and her cousin went to watch Justyn Hugh fight at Newport Leisure Centre. As coach to Hugh, Tony was working the corner that night and left his jacket behind with the words 'St Joseph's Gym' printed on the back.

Emma, who worked at the centre at the time, put a call out for the owner via social media - never has the Welsh-ism 'Whose coat is that jacket?' ever been so instrumental in bringing two people together! And the rest, as they say, is history!

Like most couples they've had their ups and downs, but there is an ease between them and a propensity to mutually support each other, and nothing demonstrated this more than when Emma lost her beautiful daughter in a terrible road accident.

Xana was Emma's second eldest child and she was just nineteen years old when tragedy struck on that terrible morning on 9th January 2015.

The loss of this vibrant young life whose dream was to eventually work in the beauty industry tore the heart out of Emma, but she still had three other children to look after and in the dark days that followed, Megan's boy became her pillar of strength.

Anyone who knows Tony will agree that he's a man who is not given to emotional displays – unless you press the 'wrong button'. But he is not without compassion, nor was he beyond tears on that dreadful day; the first and only time Emma ever saw him express emotion so openly.

As her world continued to rock on its foundations, Tony assumed his usual calm demeanour and kept her steady. The accident and the loss of Xana had a massive impact on their lives. But it also drew them closer together.

The funeral was held in St Woolos Cathedral and was attended by a huge crowd all wanting to show their respect for the short, but vivaciously-lived life of an extraordinary girl whose personality had touched so many.

Before this cataclysmic event Emma had completed her first term studying 'Learning Disability Nursing' at the

University of South Wales. Naturally, in view of her bereavement, she had been told there was no rush to return until she was good and ready. But after several weeks at home struggling to come to terms with everything that had happened, Emma needed something to focus on and resumed her studies.

Life was different for both Tony and Emma, and after four years together Megan's boy finally came to a decision. It was time to settle down.

The date was New Year's Eve 2015, the venue, Butlins in Minehead. It was the usual annual gathering, and as the couple sat amidst their large circle of friends, Tony suggested a game of 'Chinese Whispers'. He leaned in to the person next to him and the game began.

By the time it came around to Emma, all eyes were on her and there was an expectant hush. The message that had gone around was, *Tony and Emma are getting married.*

It was Tony's way of proposing, but being well-versed in his mischievous ways, Emma refused to take it seriously.

Megan's boy was never more serious, however, and some months later as they sat in their local sports club, he told her to go and enquire about some dates for an engagement party. Still unsure of his intentions, Emma decided to play it safe and brought the stewardess over with the club diary.

It was the moment of proof, and now having been well and truly put on the spot, Tony didn't disappoint and a date was set for 15th August 2017.

A trip to Birmingham then saw the purchase of a ring, and as word spread the news was greeted with a mixture of delighted surprise. *Megan's boy was tying the knot!*

By now Emma was a qualified nurse having passed all her exams with flying colours - no mean achievement and a testament to her inner strength. Following her graduation, she had been presented with two job offers and decided on a post at a secure psychiatric unit near Abergavenny. Both have come a long way and the next stage in their relationship marked a huge turning point neither could have envisaged when they first met in that taxi twenty years ago.

The big day took place at the prestigious St Pierre Hotel and Golf Club near Chepstow on 6th May 2018, and the weather couldn't have been better as family and friends came together for this momentous occasion.
As they waited for the bride they were treated to a rendition of classic love songs, courtesy of the singing skills of Rob Turley and his brother Matthew.
The atmosphere was buoyant but relaxed, until it soon became clear that the Emma was running more than traditionally late. As the registrar fluttered and the film crew tweaked their equipment, the groom remained sanguine on the surface, but there must have been a moment of doubt as he signaled for another song.
Suddenly there was a flurry of activity and then all concern melted away as the reason for the delay became apparent.
The car that had been booked for this date with destiny had failed to arrive, leaving the mother of the bride and all of the bridesmaids more frantic than the bride herself! For Emma, no stranger to the wild cards that life can throw had remained calm and unruffled as alternative transport was arranged. And when she finally made her entrance nearly an hour later, it was well worth the wait.
She looked stunning, and as she made her way up the red carpet towards her husband-to-be, Tony, in his inimitable way, tapped his wristwatch and any tension there may have been in the room fell away.
Attended by close friends and family, all eyes were on the couple, as amidst much giggling between them they took

their vows – because this is the true face of Tony and Emma;
informal, unaffected, and firmly rooted in 'themselves'
despite the film crew and photographers around them.
Their sense of fun made for an unforgettable ceremony –
particularly for the registrar – and then it was done.
Megan's boy had finally done it. He'd tied the knot! And as
they posed for endless photographs, the film crew recording
every move, there was absolutely no doubting their profound
happiness and love for each other.
After a sumptuous meal and a hilarious speech from Best
Man Roger Williams. Master of Ceremony and Corner-man
Billy kept the laughter going before Tony made a brief
speech imbued with his usual humour.
Then there was a moment, when Emma, who insisted that
she too, be allowed a speech, paid tribute to the two people
who could not be with them on this happiest of days. As she
made a toast in memory of Xana and Tony's mother -
Megan's boy looked visibly moved as everyone raised their
glass.
It was a candid and poignant reminder of just how much
their loved ones are missed and remain close to their heart.
And the love didn't stop there...

As we all know, traditionally the bride and groom take to the
floor for the first dance – alone.
But not with these two!
As they glided out to the dulcet tones of Luther Vandross's
'Never too much' - across the microphone suddenly came
the most extraordinary announcement;

*Tony and Emma would like all of their family and friends to
join them in their first dance!*

At this unprecedented display of 'one love' the guests

looked at each other uncertainly before following the lead of the Maid-of-Honour as the dance-floor began to fill up creating yet another amazingly poignant moment.
Indeed, the whole day was amazing and was made all the more special for the naturalness, simplicity, and warm generosity that the bride and groom brought to the day and their guests.

As life becomes busier with Tony's rising profile, both he and Emma face each challenge as a team. The similarities in their background mean they share a common ground and enjoy the simple things in life with little interest in the material. They both work hard, juggling their families and making time for each other.
Being under such scrutiny would be more than most people could handle, but Tony and Emma take it all in their stride and look only to enjoy the journey. Emma understands and respects Tony's passion, as he in turn appreciates her independent spirit and refusal to give in.

It was Tony's request that the final round of this book be dedicated to the wedding and their coming together. It is an acknowledgement of who he is now, and where he sees his life going. It is also a lasting and undeniable tribute to the woman he loves as finally, after all these years, Megan's boy has found his match.

Just two days after tying the knot Tony received a surprise telephone call bearing the most incredible news. His achievements had not gone unnoticed – a testament to all the blood, sweat and sheer hard work that has marked his career. More poignantly still is the fact he received the news on what would have been Megan's 83rd birthday.

Tony is modest in his pride of what he has achieved. Sometimes you get the sense he can't quite believe how far he's come from that heady first visit to Benny Jacob's gym all those years ago. But the unstinting support of his mother ensured he stuck to the path, ever striving to do better and he never lost hope – even in the darkest of times.

When the family were together in Tremorfa, Megan took great pride in her 'best room' and no one was allowed to go in it except on special occasions. Within it sat a large cabinet that displayed the many shields and trophies her son had won. Every Sunday she would take out and lovingly polish each one, no doubt dreaming of the day her feisty young warrior would surpass even her wildest wishes and make his mark.

And so he has...

On 16th September of this year (2018) Tony was inducted into the British Ex-Boxers Hall of Fame – an incredible achievement and a most prestigious honour that will ensure his name will go on.
He may not have had the boxing career he always wanted – or fulfilled his ambition to become a World Champion – but he kept faith in his own abilities and made the dream possible for others. Selflessly, determinedly and with no small amount of passion, he has shown himself to be Megan's boy through and through – and what mother wouldn't be proud of that!

ABOUT THE AUTHOR

I am a multi-genre author and enjoy writing about the things people least expect me to! I arrived very late on the literary scene having suffered with the dreaded writer's block for over 30 years!

I'm making up for lost time, however, with no less than 4 books penned and published in 2 years. You can find them all on Amazon and with 5 star reviews.

This is my first biography but I have more books planned and would like to thank 'Megan's boy' for having given me this opportunity.

.

38588230R00070

Printed in Great Britain
by Amazon